CAREERS

VAULT CAREER GUIDE TO

VENTURE CAPITAL

VENTURE
CAPITAL

BY OLEG KAGANOVICH, JAMES CURRIER,
JOE BEL BRUNO and the staff of vault

Library of Congress CIP Data is available.

ISBN 13 : 978-1-58131-610-0

ISBN 10 : 1-58131-610-0

Printed in the United States of America

ACKNOWLEDGMENTS

We are extremely grateful to Vault's entire staff for all their help in the editorial, production and marketing processes. Vault also would like to acknowledge the support of our investors, clients, employees, family and friends. Thank you!

Table of Contents

Introduction

Much has changed in the venture capital field since the go-go internet days of the late 1990s, when it seemed that any dot com business plan attached to a twenty-something entrepreneur could get funding to the tune of millions of dollars. Those days are undeniably over. But the business of venture capital has not only matured, but proven itself here to stay and ready to rebound. Consider that a group of sophomores at Harvard University launched social networking web site Facebook.com just three years ago, and it has become one of the top ten-most heavily trafficked spots on the internet. Facebook reportedly turned down a $750 million offer to buy the company in 2007, and Wall Street analysts believe it could now fetch as much as $2 billion. That's a big payoff for the Silicon Valley venture capital firms—including San Mateo, Calif.-based Greylock Partners—that initially pumped a mere $25 million into the idea.

This recent boom and bust cycle was just the latest blip in the history of investment cautionary tales, from Holland's tulip mania of the 1600s, to England's South Seas bubble of the 1700s, to Florida's real estate in the 1920s. With the dot com flameouts behind us, and the bull market halted in its tracks, Wall Street is focused again on business fundamentals. Venture capital firms are being more selective about deals—instead of competing for any half-baked business plan or investment prospect, they are scrutinizing every pre-screened deal that comes across their desks. But that doesn't mean the coffers of venture capital funds are anywhere near getting dry.

Holding steady?

The amount venture capital firms invested in private equity from 2000 through 2007 was several times more than the previous 10 years combined. And recent statistics from the National Venture Capital Association and Thomson Financial show that last year's fundraising reached its highest level since 2001. Venture capitalists raised $38.8 billion from 318 funds in 2007, with $9.7 billion of that amount sunk into early-stage ideas. Consider that just three years earlier 173 venture capital funds raised $17.3 billion. (Reality check: In the year 2000, approximately 635 funds raised over $106 billion dollars.) Though venture capital is well off its heyday, there was recently a comeback in play: over the past year, the average size of each deal closed is on the upswing. Last year, the average dollar amount of deals funded approached $8 billion—up from $7.4 billion in 2006 and $6.8 billion in 2003. Of course, it still remains to be seen how the Wall Street crisis that exploded in September 2008 will play out in the finance world.

There's no question that venture capitalists have pulled back from the funding frenzy that hallmarked the dot com boom. Until this most recent crisis, the bull market's unprecedented run had left many of these funds flush with cash and ready to inject in the next biotech or internet sensation to come along. Unlike 2000, this time around venture capital dollars are searching out good ideas with a more sober approach, and this will continue to be the case as the markets remain unsettled.

CAREERS

THE SCOOP

VENTURE CAPITAL

What is Venture Capital?

CHAPTER 1

This chapter will look at the history of venture capital as well as how venture capital activity reflects and responds to economic cycles.

A History of VC

Traditionally, individuals, families, or groups of people in tightly knit communities have invested money in private companies in the U.S. In the 1960s, a few wealthy individuals in California took to investing their money in early—stage technology companies. These people were "angels." Returns on investments were excellent. Angels began to systematically search for and invest in companies. In 1971, three of these successful angels raised additional funds from other rich individuals and institutions and placed the money in the early "venture capital funds."

On the East Coast in the late 1950s, a few formal venture investment firms began to arise. One such pioneering firm was American Research and Development Corp., envied for its investment in Digital Equipment Corp. (Later bought by Compaq in 1998, which subsequently was snapped up by Hewlett—Packard in 2002). Venture capital firms suffered a temporary downturn in 1974, when the stock market crashed and investors were naturally wary of the new kind of investment fund. In 1975, only one venture capital fund raised money, but that was the same year Tandem Computer took $1 million from a venture capital firm. Returns were tremendous for the few firms in the business in the late 1970s.

Growing possibilities

The federal government lent a helping hand in the form of legislation through this period. In 1978, the government changed the pension plan rules under ERISA (the Employee Retirement Income Security Act), making it possible for pension funds to invest in alternative (and potentially higher risk) asset classes such as venture capital firms. Pension funds represented billions of dollars in capital, so an allocation of even 1 percent of funds represented an enormous increase in the pool of money available to venture capitalists. The industry raised $750 million in 1978.

In 1979, capital gains taxes were reduced from 49 percent to 28 percent, so anyone making profits from investing in venture capital firms, or any venture capital firms making profits from investing in private companies, had to pay less taxes. In 1981, the capital gains tax was further reduced from 28 percent to 20 percent.

Then came 1983—the year of excess. The stock market peaked and there were over 100 initial public offerings (IPO) for the first time in U.S. history. That year venture capital investments jumped to a total of $4 billion. Some of 1983's funding went to newly founded companies that are some of today's largest and most prominent firms including Apple Computer and Intel.

Due to the excess of IPOs and the inexperience of many venture capital fund managers, VC returns were very low through the 1980s. In 1984, 45 new venture capital firms were formed and a long decline in returns and capital raised began. The number of new VCs declined every year through 1991, when the industry actually saw 17 more VC firms go out of business than were formed. As the public markets began to falter, opportunities dried up for private investors to liquidate their portfolios. A handful of VC firms then lead the way in trimming their funds to smooth out returns by easing the burden placed on partners to allocate large dollar amounts over fewer deals. In 1991, disbursements from the venture capital firms to their investors hit a 10—year low. VC firms retrenched, working hard to make their portfolio companies successful. The work paid off, and returns began climbing back up.

Booming into the 90s

But venture capitalists couldn't take full credit for the turnaround. Macroeconomic forces helped. In the mid–to–late 1980s, interest rates were relatively high, and the price/earnings ratios in the public markets were low. Ten years later, interest rates were low, and P/Es were very high (by historical averages). Pension funds grew dramatically. In 1987, U.S. pension funds held approximately $2.5 trillion. By 1997, that number reached $7 trillion.

The booming economy made pension fund managers more comfortable allocating up to 4 percent of their capital into alternative assets. The U.S. stock market had one of its greatest run–ups in history between 1991 and early 2000. Mutual fund assets grew from $1 trillion in 1990 to over $6 trillion in 1999.

The rise of technology

By the late 1990s, venture capital funds were in full swing—taking advantage of new technology upstarts hungry for seed money. The rate of merger and acquisition activity increased dramatically, and that created more opportunities for small, venture—backed companies to exit at high prices. VC firms cashed out in droves, putting their spoils aside with hopes to funnel into a new crop of fledgling ideas. In general, 1999 and 2000 were boom years for IPOs, and venture–backed firms were particularly prominent. In 2000, 226, or nearly two–thirds of newly public companies were backed by venture capitalists according to the National Venture Capital Association. The industry also netted approximately 245 new firms that year.

It was the period that founded some of the world's biggest technology powerhouses, chief among them being search engine Google. The company was formed in a garage in 1998, and raised a total initial investment of almost $1.1 million—including $100,000 given by Sun Microsystems Inc. co–founder Andy Bechtolsheim. Others like online music file sharing service Napster secured $15 million of financing from Hummer Winblad Venture Partners, and electronic payment provider PayPal raised more than $210 million during this period. However, the good times didn't last. By 2000, the glut of technology IPOs hitting the Nasdaq and a severe correction in the stock market sent venture–backed investments into a tailspin. 2002 saw a modest 22 venture–backed IPOs that were focused heavily toward companies in the software, health care services and medical device/equipment industries. By 2003, venture capitalists pledged a mere $19.7 billion –sliced in half from the glory days of 2000.

IPOs rebound

2004 marked yet another turning point. The Dow Jones industrials began to fight its way up, rising almost 29 percent to its peak in July, 2007. And, with more money in pocket, so did the profit–seeking VC firms. They funded 3,072 deals in 2004 worth $22.9 billion, and then pumped $30 billion into nearly 4,000 deals alone the next year. Big IPOs began to make a come back, with the most prominent being Google's flotation for $85 per share in 2004. The company's dominance in the search industry eclipsed that of both Microsoft and Yahoo, and Google now has a market valuation of about $170.4 billion. That's larger then some of the nation's biggest blue chip companies, such as J.P. Morgan Chase & Co. ($162.5B), IBM ($170.2B), and Intel ($130.6B). It marked the beginning of an upswing for Wall Street that lasted three years, carried the Dow Jones industrial average passed the 13,000 mark, and gave birth to record–high IPO and M&A deals.

The robust housing market, higher consumer confidence, and a boom in IPOs pushed stocks steadily higher after Google went public. It sent the Dow through the 11,000 mark for the first time in 2006, creating even more confidence among venture capitalists. Venture capital investors pumped $26.3 billion into young companies in 2006, more than they have in any other year since the end of the dot –com bubble. And, 2006 marked the biggest venture–backed tech IPO with voice–over–Internet–Protocol player Vonage. Things only heated up more after the Federal Reserve decided to stop raising rates in August after 17 straight hikes. Almost overnight, everyone from individual investors to businesses were relieved that costs of borrowing money would not increase. That helped foster the biggest buyout boom in history, with more than $1 trillion worth of deals done in 2006. And, 2007–driven by a surge in private equity–led buyouts—went on to break that record.

Into the present

Venture capital firms went on to raise about $29.4 billion in 2007, more than in 2006, according to the National Venture Capital Association. This was the era of social networking web sites, spawned by the success of Facebook. Microsoft approached Facebook in September 2007, proposing an investment in return for a 5 percent stake in the company. The software giant offered to pay an estimated $300 to $500 million for the stake, but later announced that it had bought a 1.6 percent share of Facebook for $246 million. There were also reports that Hong Kong billionaire Li Ka–shing invested $60 million in Facebook that year.

The new interest in social networking web sites appeared to be the next big thing for venture capitalists, and investors were clamoring to get in on what some felt would be the next Google. That burst of enthusiasm proved short lived. The second half of 2007 saw the rise of a global credit crisis that knocked the Dow'ssteady advance, and caused investors to put their money on the sidelines. With fears about a possible recession, VC firms began to alter their strategy. Yet again, the industry faced another high point—like in 2000– and began positioning themselves in 2008 toward a more cautious investing style. At the end of 2008, with a recession all–but–confirmed, VC firms will once again have to rethink their approach.

What Goes Up Must Come Down

It's no secret that the U.S. economy goes through cycles, and is now in the midst of another correction. Everything from housing prices to stock valuations tend to get overheated, or overly depressed, and that leads to a cyclical shift in sentiment. Wall Street tends to develop momentum that can last two to three years, and investors of all classes use these patterns to engage in the proverbial "buy low and sell high." The same goes for venture capitalists. The good news is that VC firms expect to nurture start–ups for up to five years, and that makes them somewhat less worried about short–term economic turbulence. However, a downturn in the economy means venture capitalists change course. Their strategy drastically shifts into what kind of upstart companies are safe to invest into, and others to be avoided. The key to understanding this shift is by poring over the most recent batch of industry data, and experts say this is paramount for anybody looking to join venture capital's ranks.

Spend or entrench

In good times, VC firms will sink billions of dollars into any business proposal that could become the next Google or Facebook. They are willing to take a gamble and pump money into ideas that could lead to a splashy initial public offering, and cash in by converting their investments into major stock holdings. That doesn't end entirely when the economy begins to slip. Instead, venture capitalists tend to entrench—picking deals at a slower and more targeted pace. VC firms, like investment banks and big private equity shops, are designed to make money in the midst of all kinds of economic conditions. A pullback in the U.S. might mean a surge of new deals overseas, one sector's glut could mirror the rise of another. Looking to secure a job as a VC analyst? Want to scout out the next blockbuster deal? Then bone up on the most recent data out there.

By the first quarter of 2008, indications were that venture capitalists had scaled back their deal–making activity, but that doesn't mean the entire industry is locked up. Despite the slipping economy, VC firms sunk $7.1 billion into 922 deals during the first three months of the year, according to the MoneyTree Report. This is a decline from both the $7.8 billion raised during the fourth quarter and $7.5 billion raised in the same quarter last year. The drop wasn't unexpected considering the global credit crunch that has paralyzed global equity markets. And the industry hasn't been helped amid further anxiety from the worst housing slump in decades that has caused a wave of defaults in subprime mortgages. The biggest downside for venture capital is that the economic environment has drastically curbed the appetite for IPOs and mergers and acquisitions—two of the biggest ways VC firms cash in on their investments.

That doesn't mean deals still aren't being done. To the contrary, insiders say investment activity remains high and that the industry is still faring better than it did after the last economic slowdown in 2001. John Taylor, vice president of research for the National Venture Capital Association, said the industry remains interested in new projects "albeit with a sense of caution." During the first quarter, 294 business plans were accepted among companies given funding for the first time. "The industry is still taking on new projects and it's consistent with what we've done in recent quarters," he said.

Follow the money ...

The best way to determine what VC firms are interested in these days is by examining the latest batch of deal data. The first quarter's smaller average deal size—$7.7 million, down from $8.8 million—means that entrepreneurs whose ideas were funded didn't need as much money. It also reflects a greater caution among venture capitalists for brand new pitches, and indicates they are interested in funding proposals for companies with more of a track record. That means those seeking a spot at a venture capital firm should be more tuned into companies that have been around awhile, and not those unnamed few struggling to get funding while operating out of some entrepreneur's garage. The numbers say as much: Companies that have not received venture capital funding in the past saw a decline in activity during the first quarter. First–stage financings totaled $1.64 billion during the period, down 27 percent from the $2.24 billion in the fourth quarter and down 4 percent from the $1.7 billion during the same period last year. Early–stage investments totaled $1.66 billion for the first quarter, down 17 percent from the fourth quarter. Early–stage investing activity accounted for 23 percent of all VC activity for the recent period compared to 26 percent in the previous period.

Breaking it down further, try to find out where VC firms are investing. Follow the money flow, and be able to talk about the latest investment trends when you meet face–to–face with a possible employer. In an industry all about making money, being able to pinpoint an area to invest despite a slowing economy is a major selling point. For instance, biotechnology and software accounted for the largest share of venture capital dollars in the first quarter. Those firms that zeroed in on biotech raised $1.27 billion in funding during the first quarter, though that was largely flat with the previous period. VC firms that focused on the software industry raised $1.26 billion, down from $1.39 billion in the previous quarter.

Following the money trail uncovers some more clues about what venture capitalists are investing in lately: the so–called "clean technology" industry. Bio–fuels and solar energy have become big business as energy prices scream to new heights. Clean–tech investments accounted for some of the largest deals in 2008. Range Fuels Inc., an ethanol production firm in Colorado, raised more than $130 million in financing during the first quarter, making it the largest VC deal for the period. Suniva Inc., a maker of solar–cell technology from Atlanta, raised $50 million during the quarter. Another solar–power firm, Infinia Corp. of Washington, raised nearly $50 million during the period. Take a look at the latest data presented by the National Venture Capital Association and other venture capital organizations. It might give you the talking points needed for the next big craze to sweep Wall Street.

... and IPOs

During a downturn in the economy, it is also a good idea to monitor how the IPO market is doing. Any good venture capitalist has their eye on the prize: The ability to bring a promising young company into the public markets and make a killing when the stock shoots sky high. The recent dearth of venture–backed IPOs is a strong indicator that they are focusing on backing mid–stage companies, hoping to bring them public when the markets become more robust.

Only five start–ups backed by U.S. venture capital firms went public in the January to March period, according to the National Venture Capital Association. That's down from 31 in the fourth quarter of 2007 and 19 in the same period, a year ago. The last time so few venture–backed businesses went public was in the second quarter of 2003, with just two IPOs. The number of companies that have filed for IPOs has also plunged, another sign start–ups are shying away from initial share sales. Only 38 were in registration at the start of 2008, down from 60 at the end of last year's fourth quarter.

That means that VCs are holding their stakes in start–ups longer than ever. If you're trying to break into the industry during a downturn, it's another reason why already established companies are what is garnering the most attention. Later–stage financings accounted for 39 percent of all first–quarter rounds, up from 32 percent in the first quarter of 2007. If the IPO and M&A markets remain slow, it could force VCs to shift more funding to later–stage investments so they can keep the companies in their portfolios afloat longer. That would have a ripple effect, influencing everything from how many new start–ups VC firms can fund, to the size of the payouts. It shows that VC firms will keep investing despite the market's weakness, adding precautions to guarantee young companies get a grasp on hiring and other spending.

Looking overseas

Want to impress them even more? Talk about the potential of investing overseas, especially in new economic gateways such as China. Last year, U.S.–based venture capitalists invested a record $1.4 billion in Asia's biggest country, according to a *MoneyTree Report* backed by PricewaterhouseCoopers and the National Venture Capital Association. That's only supposed to increase, and already some of America's leading companies are investing heavily in China Inc.

Intel Corp. this year formed a $500 million China fund to more than triple investments in companies in the world's biggest semiconductor market. Already this semiconductor–maker has sunk money into China's Holdfast Online Technology Co. and Newauto Video Technology Inc., two Chinese companies the Santa Clara, Calif.–based tech giant hopes will become the next big thing. By comparison, its previous Chinese VC fund spent $200 million in more than 28 companies. China is the world's fastest–growing major economy. And Intel, like other companies, is vying to gain a bigger share of the business boom. As are other venture capital funds. Since 1991, Intel Capital has invested more than $7.5 billion in about 1,000 companies across as many as 45 countries. Many American companies are injecting investments worth billions of dollars into burgeoning foreign economies.

IBM Corp. recently announced that its global operations would focus on new development centers in India and Beijing as part of its global aspirations. So, while the U.S economy might be slowing, the savviest venture capitalists are spending time cultivating their business overseas. That means those hoping to enter the field must not only have a firm grasp of where the U.S. economy is heading, but also know that there are opportunities offshore that will reap big windfalls for venture capital firms. For the most part, it means budding venture capitalists must keep a watchful eye on more than just the current VC climate. Research about current trends inside the U.S. economy, the IPO market, and the overseas markets remains essential for securing that first job.

The Financial Industry and Venture Capital

CHAPTER 2

Where does VC fit into the world of finance? The financial industry can be divided into two general segments: The buy–side and the sell–side. Venture capital firms are on the buy–side because they control a fund or pool of money to spend on buying an equity interest in, or assets of, operating companies. Investment banks, brokerages and commercial banks are on the sell–side because they offer such services as floating new companies on the stock exchange or issuing new debt.

For instance, when a large company wants to sell stock an investment bank's corporate finance department handles the legal, tax, advisory, and accounting affairs of the transaction as well as the sale of those securities to institutional or individual investors. For providing these services, the investment bank receives a fee (between 2 percent and 10 percent of the money raised by selling stock). An investment banking firm's primary motivation is to sell such services, characterizing them as sell–siders. Meanwhile, major brokerages are paid a fee for the service of buying and selling stocks. Commercial banks get in on the action for managing deposit accounts, making and then managing loans, etc. Again, they sell these services, so they are sell–side firms.

For the sake of this discussion, most buy–side venture capital firms have only one way to realize a return on their investment: Selling their ownership stake to another private investor, a corporation (trade sale) or to the public markets for more money than they paid (often termed to be "in the money"). Private equity shops like Blackstone Group or Kohlberg, Kravis Roberts sink their money into later–stage companies with the hopes of cashing out in a public offering. Venture capital is about building young companies and finding an exit (liquidity event) on the back side for "x" times their original investment. Descriptions of each segment of the buy–side are included below. Keep in mind that these definitions are intended to be very general in nature and that many buy–side organizations cross organizational boundaries.

Friends and family

Sometimes referred to as "friends, family and fools," this is usually the first source of funding for startups at the idea stage of development. The amounts invested per individual are quite small, averaging $5,000 to $10,000. These people may not have an in–depth understanding of the business, product, technology or market, and are simply making an investment in someone they know. While this is probably the easiest money for an entrepreneur to find, it can also be bittersweet. If a startup fails, telling Aunt Edna that she's lost her nest egg could be the low point of one's career.

Angels

These are high net–worth individuals who normally invest between $15,000 and $1 million in exchange for equity in a young company throughout the seed and early stage rounds, averaging $50,000 to $500,000. Angels prefer to invest within their immediate geographic area, and on average within one day of travel. According to businessfinance.com, angels fund an estimated one–seventh of the 300,000 start–up/early growth firms in the U.S. They are often the first investor segment who has the opportunity to sit on the board of directors and contribute experience and contacts, guiding young companies through the difficult initial stages of growth. That said, most of the value added by angel investors occurs in the pre–institutional (or Series A) rounds of funding. As the professional investors come into play, venture capitalists take over board seats previously held by angels.

Angels can be doctors, lawyers, former investors, though increasingly they are former entrepreneurs who have had a lucrative exit in their chosen professional field. Microsoft co–founder and multi–billionaire Paul Allen has made headlines for his angel investing as well as his investments through his VC firm, Vulcan Ventures. Intel co–founder Andy Grove has made angel investments in numerous companies, including Oncology.com. Given the large number of new companies seeking funding as well as the rise in the number of wealthy individuals, in recent years the industry has seen the emergence of angel groups. These investor alliances create more structure for angel investors, and a more efficient conduit for moving startups along from seed funding to professional venture investors. Perhaps the best–known group of angels is Silicon Valley's "Band of Angels," a formal group of about 150 former and current high tech entrepreneurs and executives who meet monthly to consider pleas from three start–ups for venture financing. This group has injected more than $100 million across some 150 startups.

Angels are often involved with hiring, strategy, the raising of additional capital, and fundamental operating decisions. These alliances also allow for better coordination of due diligence in "vetting" new deals. Angels are not without their own issues, however. Collectively, angel investors have been accused of being fair weather friends; one of the first sources of private equity to dry up when public markets fall or macroeconomic conditions deteriorate. With less money to invest across fewer deals than their VC brethren, many of these individuals have a lower tolerance for losses. This risk aversion is compounded by their generally lower position in the capital structure. While angel groups may be able to negotiate preferred stock instead of common, their equity rarely has the same level of preferences or security demanded by later stage investors. Though angels, of course, expect a significant return on their investment, they are also thrill–seekers of a sort—motivated by getting close to the excitement of a new venture.

High-net-worth private placements

Investment banks such as industry leader Goldman Sachs Group Inc. that represent the sell–side of a deal may organize a group of very wealthy individuals, corporations, asset management firms, and/or pension funds to make a direct investment into a private company. These funds typically raise between $5 million and $50 million—sometimes in the billions for funds managed by some of Wall Street's biggest names. In essence, they enable a broad swath of institutional and wealthy private investors to put their money to work like major venture capital firms.

While these transactions may include a traditional venture fund as part of the round, in many cases they do not. As a whole, investment banks have historically been seen as having less perceived value in the early stages of the venture process. Since early–stage investing is not Wall Street's core competency, the downside is that the startup company may not benefit from the expertise, operational savvy, and rolodex of the venture capital firm. While there is a credible value proposition to using private placements and participation by investment banks in funding some types of deals, this is expensive money on several fronts.

Asset management firms and pension funds

These groups include a diverse collection of limited partnerships and corporations that manage between $5 million to $100 billion plus. Most focus on diversified investment strategies, typically with public instruments including stocks, bonds, commodities, currencies, etc. They rarely invest in private companies, due to the large amount of time required to find and execute a private transaction, as well as the ongoing commitment of time to monitor such an investment. Instead of directly participating in individual startup fundings, many will allocate 5 to 7 percent of total funds to higher–risk alternative investments like VC partnerships, hedge funds and distressed turnaround situations. The California Public Employees' Retirement System (CalPERS) is one of the largest players in this space. As of September 2007, their AIM (Alternative Investment Management) Program had total investment exposure of $42.6 billion. Since its inception in 1990, the program has generated $12.5 billion in profit.

Private equity firms

Consider private equity firms to be the bigger, badder version of venturecapital. They rarely involve themselves in upstart companies, but certainly have their eye on opportunity. Big PE firms like Blackstone and KKR have entire departments empowered to invest seed money into the next big internet phenomenon. However, their main strategy is to buy vulnerable publicly–traded companies that can hand them a huge profit. The strategy: Find an under–performing public company, take them private and then reorganize them using loans. That's why it is called leveraged finance. And the big payoff for LBOs is when they make money bringing them public again. For instance, private equity fund Cerberus Capital is now in the process of reorganizing Chrysler—an American icon it bought from German car titan Daimler AG (famous for its Mercedes brand). Once turned around, Chrysler should reap big financial rewards for Cerberus if the automaker goes public.

Hedge funds

These are entities that buy and sell public market instruments including stocks, bonds, commodities, currencies, etc. These firms take bets on market fluctuations to make money, and are often considered high risk/high return investors. The size of these funds ranges from a few million to several billion dollars. They care about making quick money.

Trading

Sell–side companies such as merchant banks, commercial banks and investment banks have trading departments that control and invest huge sums of money into public markets. These groups also take relatively risky bets on market fluctuations.

Venture funds

Limited partnerships are described at length later in the book.

Industry Trends

The internet boom of the 1990s sent the number of venture capital firms surging, and the amount of money they raised hit astronomical heights. Almost any idea, even from companies that had never seen a profit, were open game as VC firms hoped for the best in a no–can–lose atmosphere. Much has changed in the years since. Even in 2007, when Wall Street seem unstoppable and market indexes hit new heights, the venture capital industry continued to struggle. But there were signs of life. Thomson Financial and the National Venture Capital Association reported that 235 venture funds raised money in 2007, a 2.6 percent increase from 2006. The amount of money raised climbed 9.4 percent to $35 billion year over year. In a statement, Mark Heesen, president of the NVCA, said that clean technology and life science businesses, in particular, require substantial capital investment. Heesen said the industry is "nowhere near the unsustainable fundraising levels" of 1999 to 2001, when more than $200 billion gushed into VC funds.

Venture fundraising has steadily gained momentum since the bust year of 2002, when 179 funds raised $3.9 billion. In 2003, limited partners doubled their venture investing to $10.6 billion and 2004 saw another sharp increase to $19.1 billion. The $11 billion raised in the fourth quarter was the biggest haul since $14.2 billion flowed to venture firms in the second quarter of 2006. However, investments in start–ups fell 5 percent to $7.1 billion during the first three months of 2008 compared to the year–ago quarter, signaling that venture capitalists may be less willing to open their wallets during a U.S. economic downturn.

Great expectations

Prior to the latest crisis, things had been looking up for venture capital investors. IPOs, which provide the biggest opportunity for VCs to cash out, were continuing to recover from their mid–decade doldrums. The biggest boost came December 20, 2007 when software maker NetSuite (NYSE: N) raised $161 million in its highly anticipated public flotation—a signal that 2008 was making a comeback. And the median buyout price of venture–backed companies was continuing to rise. Riding that momentum, venture capitalists expected 2008 to be the year that they would finally start to unload companies in their portfolios that have been absorbing cash for years. A survey of 170 VCs released by the National Venture Capital Association at the end of 2007 showed that 59 percent of venture investors expected the market for IPOs to strengthen in 2008. Nearly three–quarters expected M&A transaction values—already nearly double 2005 levels—to either increase or remain the same in 2007. The internet, clean technology and life sciences companies remain some of the key areas.

It's not that VC has developed an appetite for more mature later–stage opportunities that have been attractively priced over the past few years. We aren't saying that early–stage investing has gone away. Simply put, the depressed "seller's market" since the tech boom has created an overabundance of later–stage already–funded companies that were being given valuations similar to those of their more risky start–up cousins. With longer track records and many more milestones reached in their march toward profitability and a successful exit, these later stage investment opportunities have posed stiff competition for new companies that might be looking for funding.

Traditional venture capital firms are accompanied by the venture capital activity of huge corporations such as Intel and Microsoft, with more recent splashes made by corporate titans Johnson & Johnson, Merck, Novartis, Eli Lilly and GlaxoSmithKline PLC. These monoliths have learned how to make minority investments while allowing the invested companies freedom to compete effectively through corporate venture programs and strategic investment groups. It wasn't always thus—in the past, large corporations were reluctant to invest in companies they didn't control, and their VC operations often came and went. The old greenhouse model (of seeding new technologies/ventures internally) used by Baby Bells, Corning, Xerox, IBM and Teradyne has given way to a newer model that closely parallels the investing strategies of the VC firms, and is proving much more successful.

Because of the market downturn over the past several years, however, many corporations are curtailing their corporate VC investments to some degree. That said, those who are still (or newly) in the fray are spending money (some more than ever) on software, semiconductors, bioinformatics, biotech, medical devices, and security technologies. The products within these industries range from facial recognition software, to more efficient drug delivery systems, to minimally–invasive medical technologies used during surgery.

Startup strategy

So what does this mean for the current state of entry–level stage startups?

Darwin may not have been far off of the mark. The young start–ups that are getting funded (and sometimes even oversubscribed back in the day) have proven management teams, low burn rates, unique (dependable) intellectual property, business models that make sense and real customers who are desperate for their products. While it is true that fewer new companies are getting funded (than had been five years ago), the investment dollars spent today are being spread amongst the top contenders. Silicon Valley venture capitalist Warren Packard sums it up, "We now have more time to play with, so [we] can invest deeper into intellectual property. Where in the past a $3 million investment was expected to last for six months, we might look for $2 million to carry a start–up through several years. We are willing to fund companies at a very low burn rate."

As the uncertainty in the economy refuses to go away, venture firms are establishing stronger relationships with angels, the former entrepreneurs who got rich during the last decade of explosive growth in the stock market. (In 1999, for example, Sendmail, a hot start–up, opted to take financing from The Band of Angels instead of some top VC firms.) Angel investment has declined alongside corporate VC programs, as many angels have seen their wealth contract significantly. However, with a penchant for entrepreneurial activity and expertise in early stage company growth, angel investors have a strong role to play as the money bridge between "friends and family" and venture capitalists.

Organizational changes

The organizational structure of venture capital firms is evolving. In the past few years, VC firms have been employing more associates—sub–partner personnel. (This is a good thing for eager MBAs attempting to enter the competitive venture capital industry.) Most firms had little support other than their own network of professional contacts out in the community. Then companies like Summit Partners, TA Associates, and Battery Ventures built effective, high–return VC firms by relying upon junior level personnel. Associates became experts in niche markets, providing value with the sheer depth of their understanding.

Combining deep, narrow knowledge from associates and broad business and strategic knowledge from general partners has proved to be a very effective model. Another organizational change to VCs has resulted from the trend of venture capital firms to become more proactive in ensuring the success of their investments. Some sizable VCs are adding early stage functional experts to their firms in areas like mergers and acquisitions, executive recruiting, public relations, market research and operations. These in–house personnel allow the venture capital firms to add more value, assert more control over the life of the investment, and increase the possibility that the portfolio companies become bottom–line boons.

Organizations and publications such as Dow Jones' Venture One (www.ventureone.com) and VentureWire (www.venturewire.com), The Deal (www.thedeal.com); and The National Venture Capital Association (www.nvca.com) provide a great deal of analysis about the macro trends in the industry, current deal financings and issues of the day. They keep track of how much capital has been invested in VC funds each year, how much was deployed from those funds into companies each year, into which areas of the country and into which industry segments the money was deployed, what the rates of return on those investments have been and so on.

The Nuts and Bolts of Venture Capital

CHAPTER 3

Stages of Venture Capital Investment

Venture capital firms invest in five different stages of a company's growth. Keep in mind that the numbers below are often industry specific. A seed or start–up round for a capital intensive business like semiconductors may require millions, whereas a software company may only need start–up funding of $100,000. These stages are general guidelines, and may sometimes overlap.

Seed

This is the initial stage: When an investment of between $1,000 and $500,000 is made in a company's embryonic stage. This involves a handful of people with an idea and little or no revenue and/or a start–up investment of between $50,000 and $1 million in private companies that are completing product development and beginning initial marketing. For example, a divorced mother has an idea to start a social networking web site for others in the same situation. The site isn't even running yet, but she has a business plan for www.singleparents.com and is looking for someone to give her the money needed to get started. She'll look for seed money from venture capitalists willing to take a chance at a very preliminary stage.

Early stage (also called first stage, first institutional round, first letter round, Series A)

An investment of between $1,000,000 and $15 million is made when a company has completed its product but has unimpressive revenues. At this point, the start–up may have trial customers accounting for a sizable portion of its revenue. Following the previous example, the entrepreneur has the social networking web site up and running in beta. The new company already has had initial investment, and operates like a small business with designs to expand on a national or global scale. The added venture capital dollars has allowed singleparents.com to hire a small staff—sales positions, graphic artists, writers and others—and open an office to base operations out of.

Later stage (also second stage, series B)

An investment of between $2 million and $15 million is made when a firm has a successful product and revenue, and has often already taken money from other institutional investors. After benefiting from early–stage investment, the web site for divorced parents has a growing amount of subscribers and is luring an increasing amount of online advertisers. This next tranche of cash allows them to push even farther by opening bigger headquarters, hire more staff needed for a major expansion, beef up advertising and buy the needed servers and computer equipment to handle the rush of new subscribers. At this point the company has become so successful that the press is buzzing about it and singleparents.com has the attention of Wall Street"s army of investment bankers.

Mezzanine (also third stage, growth stage)

An investment of between $2 million and $20 million is made into a company for a major expansion, generally leading to an initial public offering in three to 18 months. Singleparents.com now has a chief executive, a president and a chief financial officer. The company has shown a steady record of revenue, and kept expenses down to show a strong profit. This is a web site that is at the top of its game, routinely mentioned as the "next big thing," and has even become part of the American lexicon like "Google it" or "Facebook me." This is about the time that those venture capital funds that passed on seed, early stage, and late stage financings begin to kick themselves. An IPO is certainly in the offing.

Bridge

Often, the term "bridge financing" is used to describe a speedy financing of a company that is in trouble and needs some more time to get to a more substantial round of financing.

But sometimes a bridge financing is a bridge to an IPO. In this case, "bridge" refers to an investment between $2 million and $20 million made three to 12 months before the company goes public. ("Going public" means it issues equity shares available for purchase by the public.) Another common way to say "going public" is "IPO." The company is typically profitable at this stage. Back in the heyday of the internet craze, internet companies were able to generate enough support to list their shares without even being public. Shareholders were eager to buy into the next big thing, and that emboldened them to overlook any balance sheet problems. Those days, however, are gone for now.

There are several reasons a company might take on a round of bridge financing just prior to its public flotation (when it would presumably raise a lot of money). It may want to bolster its books in order to be more attractive to investors. The company alternatively might want to snare a prestigious board member/investor or in order to increase its stock value. Finally, some companies may want to hedge their bets in case of a failed IPO.

Banks and other institutions often supply bridge financing for upstart companies, sometimes in exchange for taking a bigger role later on when that company goes public. However, the credit freeze in late 2007 made many investment banks more selective about where their capital is used. Bridge financings have not dried up completely, but fledgling companies can't get them with the same ease they once could.

The "Capital" in Venture Capital

Where do buy–side funds get their money? Most of the money comes from pension funds. Capital is also derived from endowments of non–profit institutions such as universities and museums, foundations, insurance companies, banks and wealthy families and individual corporations. Pension funds are money set aside by corporations (typically large) for their employees' retirement. These assets pile up over the years and can amount to billions of dollars. The money must be invested so that its value will be sufficient to cover the needs of the employees at the time of retirement. To maximize return and minimize risk, the pension money is invested in many places—stocks, bonds, currencies, real estate and "alternative investments."

Typically, 5 to 7 percent of the total funds are invested into what pension fund managers call "alternative investments," and what we call the "buy–side" firms. Pension fund managers expect higher rates of return (15 to 30 percent) from these alternative asset investments, and they understand that there is a commensurately higher risk associated with such investments. The aim of the buy–side firms, including venture capital firms, is to provide high rates of return to their investors. Only by producing high rates of return can buy–side firms continue to raise money and thereby stay in business.

There is also increasing interest in providing capital to upstart companies from private equity funds. Since 2006, PE shops have cashed–in on the merger & acquisition boom. Firms like Blackstone and KKR—which have reaped massive profits in recent years—are putting their money to work by seeking out venture capital opportunities. But, like pension funds, their quest is still making a strong return. Private equity is also a savvy and patient investor. Even if the economy begins to slip, most PE firms are comfortable with sinking money into young companies—mostly because it is just a fraction of their massive cash stockpile. Again, venture capital investments are for the patient and often take four years to develop into the next IPO sensation.

Venture capital firms are therefore beholden to the pension funds, endowments and private equity firms. (Following the "golden rule" logic, the venture capital firms tend to have the upper hand with companies into which they invest.) These power relations don't always hold true. When a venture capital firm produces very high rates of return on a consistent basis, pension funds will compete to invest in it, allowing the venture firm to dictate terms. Venture capital firms may also compete to invest in a particularly hot start–up (perhaps one with a high rate of growth, or one started by a serial entrepreneur with a track record of success).

How Venture Capital Funds are Funded and Structured

The traditional venture capital fund

Most venture capital funds are set up as independent Limited Partnerships. This includes well–known coastal names like Kleiner Perkins Caufield & Byers, Draper Fisher Jurvetson, and Highland Capital Partners, as well as regional up–and–comers Akers Capital, and William Blair New World Ventures. The venture capital firm acts as the general partner (GP) with third–party institutions investing the bulk of the capital to the fund, filling the role of limited partner (LP). During the fundraising phase that every venture firm goes through in building a new fund, the GP seeks out investment commitments from accredited investors. The VC distributes a private placement memorandum (PPM) or prospectus to potential LPs, and might expect to raise the necessary capital over the course of the ensuing six to 12 months. To place this within context of the internet boom, some new funds closed within 60 to 90 days during the height of 1999–2000.

Funds generally raise anywhere from $10 million to several billion dollars from their limited partners. According to the National Venture Capital Association (NVCA), more than 50 percent of investments in venture capital come from institutional pension funds, with the balance coming from endowments, foundations, insurance companies, banks, affluent individuals and other entities who seek to diversify their portfolio with an investment in risk capital. Two hundred and thirty–five venture capital firms raised $34.7 billion in 2007, according to Thomson Financial and the National Venture Capital Association. Additionally, 2007 fundraising dollars reached the highest level seen since 2001 when venture capitalists raised $38.8 billion from 318 funds. It is the GP's job to invest this capital in privately held, high–growth companies. In order to make these investments, the venture firm has to "call in" its LPs' commitments through tranches or "capital calls." Venture firms have synchronized these calls (sometimes also called "takedowns" or "paid–in capital,") to their funding cycles, allowing funds to be available on an as–needed basis.

A partnership agreement sets forth the relationship between the GP (the VC firm) and their LPs (investors). The returns of the venture capital fund are distributed back to the LPs as dictated by the partnership agreement, but naturally lean toward the later years of the fund. The reason for the preponderance of partnerships, as opposed to corporations, is the security that partnerships give venture capitalists to make long–term decisions. Once an agreement is signed and the capital commitments are made, the LPs are generally stuck with this group of venture professionals for the duration of the partnership (VC funds are generally organized as 10–year partnerships). For the duration of the partnership, the institutional investors cannot remove their capital from the fund at will. Liquidity is realized when a viable exit option becomes available.

Liquidity options

Both IPOs and M&A transactions are credible exit strategies. However, in the current market condition, both of those strategies have begun to slow dramatically. Companies that are still flush with cash are more choosy about who they take over. And, volatile market conditions have made it much more complicated for fledgling young companies to count on a blockbuster IPO. That doesn't mean these exit strategies still aren't happening. They are, but with much more due diligence. If that happens, a liquidity event can take several forms, including a cash deal, stock, or both. Capital or shares of stock are then distributed back to investors according to the partnership agreement, unlike a mutual fund where invested cash can be withdrawn at any time. As a result however, the arrangement allows venture capitalists to act as a relatively reliable pool of risk capital. Plus, VC firms will rarely "go bankrupt." If unsuccessful, they are more likely to be wound down over time without the ability to raise an additional fund.

For example, a typical 10–year venture capital fund may cash flow something like this:

- **Year one to four:** Initial portfolio company investments are made
- **Years three through seven:** Follow–on investments are made into the portfolio companies
- **Years three through 10:** The investments are exited/liquidated.

Not unlike a mutual fund, a venture capital firm may be managing several individual funds at any given time. The individual funds are distinct entities with their own set of limited partners, although LPs do sometimes overlap across funds. As one might imagine, this creates a pile of issues that we will not try to go into here (if you really want to know how the story of VC partnership ends, both Josh Lerner and Joe Bartlett have leading books on the subject).

Distributions and carried interest

Typically, venture capital fund profits are istributed as follows: 80 percent to the LPs and 20 percent (carried interest) to the general partner after the limited partners have recovered their initial investment. During the fever paced period of 1999 and 2000, these percentages adjusted to a 70/30 split for some of the most popular and promising funds raised. To nobody's surprise, funds raised over the past several years have had a much harder time negotiating a 30 percent carry. There are as many variations on carry, distribution and similar terms as there are firms. The terms are ultimately established through negotiations on a case–by–case basis. (See the glossary and sample term sheet at the end of this guide for definitions of terms related to the venture capital industry.)

And now the government is looking into how everyone from venture capitalist, private equity and hedge funds use carried interest. The Senate Finance Committee has held hearings on the tax treatment of "carried interest." A carried interest is a right to receive a specified share (often 20 percent) of the profits ultimately earned by an investment fund without contributing a corresponding share of the fund's financial capital. It is part of the standard compensation package for managers of private equity funds. The government has accused these funds of taking advantage of a provision of current law that makes it possible for them to avoid paying corporate income taxes, even after issuing public stock. Prior to the development of this new tax strategy, nearly all publicly–traded partnerships were subject to the corporate income tax.

Management fees

The general partner (VC firm) charges a fee for its role as portfolio manager. This management fee covers the fund's costs such as rent, salaries and keeping the lights on. The fee is usually 1 to 2.5 percent of the assets, or committed capital. The actual percentage can vary based on fund size, the partners' prior investment history, etc. Although the management fee is often paid quarterly over the life of the fund, it is not uncommon for it to diminish over time (toward the end of the fund's life–cycle). Why is all this important? Because at the end of the day, this is how you get paid. That 20 percent of carry is split amongst the employees of the firm at the discretion of the managing or general partners.

Finance industry affiliate VC programs

Some venture firms are born as the affiliate or subsidiary offspring of an investment/commercial bank or insurance company (e.g. JP Morgan Partners, US Bancorp Piper Jaffray, Goldman Sachs Private Equity Group, and AIG Capital Partners). Depending upon these funds' reasons for being, they make investments on behalf of the parent firm's partners, management or wealthy clients. Others bring in outside limited partners, and run their funds no differently than any other venture capital general partnership.

Corporate venture capital programs

Corporate venture capital programs typically begin as subsidiaries or affiliates of large non–financial corporations such as Intel, Sun Microsystems, GE Capital, Microsoft and Merck. Most of these subsidiaries have a charter or mission statement which calls for making direct investments that are of "strategic" value to the parent corporation. The dynamics of how investment opportunities are found and deals get done differ from firm to firm. However, since many of these companies are publicly held, there is often a two–pronged approach to deal sourcing. The perfect corporate venture investment is one where the corporation's business unit (depending on the industry/space/etc.) champions the deal. This makes sense, since with every signed term sheet (see example at the end of the book) the corporation concludes a Memorandum of Understanding (MOU) spelling out what both the startup and the corporation itself will contribute as future partners in this relationship. As the strategic component to the investment, the business unit will be intimately involved with the portfolio company after the deal is done. If this turns out not to be the case, all of the highly touted strategic value is likely lost.

Business units of publicly held companies need to deliver the numbers every quarter, so the investments they source reflect an effort to tackle current pains. On the other hand, venture groups like Intel Capital have historically also had hard core techies on the deal team, who have the breathing room to look out at 12–18 months. They search for "cool" technologies, without being fettered by either practical current application or connection to their core business. Either way, strategic value is king.

Although it is extremely difficult to quantify said value, the objective of this investment strategy can be to fill an R&D role (buy vs. build), penetrate new markets, or help sell more core products. Over the past decade, Intel has made investments in large numbers of multimedia hardware start–ups, aware that these technologies would require progressively more powerful Intel processors. This is a clear lesson in creating demand to fuel sales. While a few of the more experienced corporate investors have a good handle on the balance between strategic value and financial return, this has been a trouble spot and point of contention with less seasoned corporate venture teams. The bias toward strategic investing has the potential to create confusion, poorly aligned goals and disincentives within/between the venture team, management, and corporate shareholders. The most probable ensuing conflicts from this and other corporate investment issues include:

1) Public for–profit corporations prioritizing strategic value in venture investments, without sufficient focus on ROI (Return on Investment)

While there is much to be said for strategic value, the point—the only point—is to make money. It is not always possible however, to calculate how an investment in a start–up today will impact Sun Microsystems' bottom line on a recurring basis three years from now. Yet as a public company, Sun's management must answer to shareholders once every quarter. So, unless the dollars invested can be demonstrably proven to either move more product or in some other way increase net income, ROI must play a more central role within corporate venture programs.

2) Companies sometimes compartmentalize their corporate venture groups.

For example, one multibillion dollar Silicon Valley corporation launched its venture program by dividing responsibilities between sourcing investments, negotiating deals, and managing the investment portfolio. This structure lends itself to lack of ownership or accountability by any one team. The sourcing group looks for the "gee–whiz" gizmo factor, with little regard for business model or financials. The deal team then has to complete enough diligence to decide whether this investment should go forward. If the decision is "no," then the team faces an uphill battle and the political repercussions of trying to kill the deal. Worse yet, portfolio start–ups are forced to work with someone new every several weeks throughout the deal negotiation and funding process.

3) Board seats are a serious liability

As we have all seen over the past several years, board members are held accountable when their company stumbles. To avoid this conflict, publicly held firms should only accept board observer status. This gives corporate investors a window into portfolio companies on a month– to– month basis, without exposing the parent corporation to litigation and undue liability.

Some corporate investors do place a strong emphasis on financial returns, and may even function purely as financial investors capitalizing on the technology, know–how, reputation, and access to capital of the parent. Players in this realm include Lucent Venture Partners, Dell Ventures and Nokia Venture Partners. While somewhat controversial, these programs can produce some of the most enviable returns in the industry, and successful programs are often spun off as separate venture funds.

Quarterly evaluations

Hundreds of venture programs have been shuttered in the past few years, with most of them closing in the immediate aftermath of the technology bubble. Others have been cut back, restarted, and cut back again. While the economy played a large role in this contraction, it has historically been difficult for corporate VCs to retain good venture capital professionals, and to stay the course when shareholders have a quarter–by–quarter view.

Nevertheless, it looks as if corporations will continue to be an increasingly important part of venture capital. We have only to look at Microsoft, Merck and Intel as leaders in the business. As other corporations have retreated or completely withdrawn from corporate investing, others have stepped up their interest in discovering and building new companies. Google is becoming a bigger force in the past two years in venture capital—and, at the same time, annoying some of the more established VC firms along the way. The search engine is scooping up upstart tech companies at a relatively bargain–basement price, giving itself new opportunities by luring entrepreneurs with its name while boxing out venture capitalists at the same time. Google has been investing about $500,000 a year to promising startups, often buying those companies afterwards, according to several media reports in 2007.

Other venture capital structures

Venture capital firms can be effective with structures other than the ones outlined above. Limited Liability Corporations (LLCs) such as Granite Ventures of San Francisco are an alternative form of structuring a fund, but for our purposes, these function in a similar manner as Limited Partnerships. The venture capital firm MVC Capital Inc., also known as meVC (NYSE: MVC), is an example of a closed end publicly traded venture fund. It is run by former KKR general partner Michael Tokarz, who added ten new investments and 16 follow–on investments, committing total capital of approximately $167.1 million.

Harris & Harris Group (NASDAQ–NM: TINY) is also a publicly held venture capital firm, operating as a Business Development Company ("BDC") under the Investment Company Act of 1940. However, its shares—like meVC—have struggled to remain in positive price–per–share territory since its debut. Both companies have been beaten down by the economy's latest dip, and investors these days are steering clear of companies tied to the markets.

Smaller alternatives

The NVCA outlines other organizations, including government– affiliated investment programs that help start up companies either through state, local or federal programs. One increasingly popular vehicle is the Small Business Investment Company (SBIC) program administered by the Small Business Administration (SBA), through which a venture firm supplements its own pool of funds with federal money at a ratio of two government dollars to every dollar raised via limited partners. Meanwhile, the SBA only requires a limited return on their investment. While SBIC funds create more paperwork and bureaucracy for the general partnership, they can be a good deal for the limited partners. Between the inflated power of their leveraged investment and limited ROI upside for the SBA, LPs in an SBIC have a good thing going during the good economic times. Don't forget however, that returns are based on timing. SBA funds require interest payments, and the GP might have to pay 6 to 7 percent when only making 10 to 12 percent annually.

Despite the endless maturations for organizing venture capital firms, atypical structures should set off a red flag for the applicant. "Why are they not a fund?" is the first question that a job–seeker should ask herself. While many alternative methods of organization have merit, a prospective applicant should be comfortable that the firm in question has sufficient unencumbered capital and is not just trying to look as if it does.

CAREERS

GETTING HIRED

VENTURE CAPITAL

The Hiring Process

CHAPTER 4

Overview

Venture capital remains a hot field, and aspiring venture capitalists have their work cut out for them. But it's not impossible to get hired in this dynamic area.

Getting started

Your first step should be to identify all possible areas in which you might be able to start a venture capital career. These include:

- Private partnerships and small, incorporated entities (prestigious and sexy, they give the industry its reputation
  - – Battery Ventures (www.battery.com)
  - – Draper Fisher Jurvetson (www.dfj.com)
  - – RRE Ventures (www.rre.com)
- Corporate venture programs or divisions of major corporations
  - – GE Equity (www.geequity.com)
  - – Intuit (www.intuit.com)
  - – Panasonic (www.panasonicventures.com)
- Affiliates of investment banks
  - – Goldman Sachs (www.goldmansachs.com)
  - – J.P. Morgan Chase (www.oneequity.com)
  - – Piper Jaffray Ventures (www.piperjaffray.com)
- Venture leasing funds are another vehicle that allow start-ups to finance certain infrastructure and equipment needs (they take equity in return for a lower rate on leased equipment or real estate). A typical transaction might involve the lease of equipment to early stage companies at a lower-than market interest rate over several years. In addition to lease payments, the lessors will often request warrants for company stock as a further incentive to mitigate the added risk in lending to a very young company.
  - – Black Emerald Capital (www.blackemerald.com/assetmanage.html)
  - – CIT Venture Leasing Fund (www.cit.com)

Direct investment activity by insurance companies, pension funds or investment advisory firms

- AIG (www.aigprivateequity.com)
  - The MONY Group (www.mony.com)
  - Wells Fargo & Company (www.wellsfargo.com)
- SBICs (for the full list, take a look at the SBA web site: www.http://sba.gov/)
  - Blue Rock Capital (www.bluerockcapital.com)
- Funds of funds (fund structures that primarily invest as LPs in multiple venture funds) and hedge funds with established venture capital teams can be a good stepping-stone. Working in these groups will give you access to the top-tier venture capitalists, and provide a solid understanding of how the business works from an LP perspective
  - CalPERS (www.calpers.com)
  - LJH Global Investments (www.ljh.com)

Gaining Exposure

The best way to learn about venture capital is by getting exposure to the world within which VCs work. The low hanging fruit here are the venture capital clubs at most business schools. There are private equity conferences across the country that open their doors (free of charge) to club volunteers who are willing to take tickets, operate audiovisual equipment, or in some other way help to facilitate a smoothly running VC conference. For those not in business school, volunteering at the conferences may also be an inexpensive entry to accessing venture capitalists. You are of course also welcome to pay the cover charge, but be prepared for the cost of admission to range from several hundred to several thousand dollars.

In meeting venture capitalists from around the country, you will quickly come to two important observations:

1) In general, East Coast VCs place a high degree of value on financial acuity and experience, while investors further west have a much stronger bias toward operational proficiency. This should be no surprise, since many Silicon Valley VCs tend to be former operators (founders and C-level

management) of extremely successful start ups from days gone by, while many Boston and New York investors get their start as investment bankersand money managers. While there are no hard and fast rules, bankers will probably have an easier time breaking into venture capital on the East Coast, whereas seasoned executive managers with deep industry experience and technical know-how will likely face better odds in California. Warren J. Packard, an active West Coast VC and Draper Fisher Jurvetson managing director, falls into the latter category. "The traditional career path to VC is to bring a host of experience to bear as a venture capitalist, be it through marketing, business development, product development, or sales. That's the ideal and traditional way to do it."

2) As one ascends (toward later stage investments) the private equity ladder, the required skill set and temperament noticeably changes. Early stage investors tend to be very entrepreneurial and operationally oriented, while later stage (mezzanine to LBO) investors live in the world of high finance and testosterone. It is therefore extremely important for anyone considering private equity as a career to understand themselves and where they would best fit along this investment continuum. "More than any deep (decades' worth of) industry knowledge," says Packard just a few years ago, "an early-stage VC's value proposition is diversity of experience. Unlike most entrepreneurs, who are all about focusing on the task at hand and drilling down to every minute detail, VCs like to think in terms of the big picture." Don't be surprised if a venture capitalist says to you, "I'm sorry. I can't remember what you were just talking about, but I've just thought of a way to change the world."

The skill set

The next step involves developing the required skill set for a venture capitalist. Some of the skills mentioned here are not required of those in junior positions, but you will be evaluated on your ability to develop theseskills over time.

Schmoozing: First and foremost, venture capital is a relationship management business. Schmooze with everyone in sight to find deals first or to latch onto hot companies. Schmoozing also comes in handy when you're doing due diligence on a company and its market—you must find the sources of information you need and then extract the appropriate information. A good network is a big success factor in any industry, but this is doubly true for venture capital. Building a big Rolodex either in a geographic region or an industry is a must.

Consulting: You need to be able to give superior strategic advice to your portfolio companies in areas such as hiring and firing, technical strategy, sales execution, distribution, growth strategy, and product mix. Your advice is one of the big "value-added" features of having a venture firm as an investor. Previous work experience as a consultant can't hurt, but is often not enough by itself.

Financial knack: A venture capitalist advises an entrepreneur on financial strategy. This requires corporate finance knowledge. A deep knowledge of accounting and hands-on experience with mergers and acquisitions are of particular value. The VC works with I-bankers when an IPO rolls around and manages large amounts of money. Excel is, as always, your friend. Industry expertise: Because you will invest in the cutting-edge companies of whatever industry may be your focus (telecom, software, biotech, consumer products, retail, health service, etc), you need to be a player in that industry to get credibility. You need to know the other hot companies, top managers, the industry history and lore, and the latest rumors and trends. This kind of knowledge is necessary to give superior advice in competitive positioning, alliances and partnerships, and executive hiring.

Operational background: You cannot be an early stage venture investor without some kind of background in operations. This can be anything from a management role in a start up, to spending several years as a marketing, sales or business development specialist for a high-tech Fortune 500 company. A well-known VC was quoted as saying, "Wouldn't it be neat if I could just spend a year selling something?"

Good judgment: Either you're born with it or you learn it by trial and error. Either way, it's necessary for savvy investment decisions. Deep rich experience is less important than strong intuition, a curious mind, and vision.

Career Path

There is no typical path for a successful career in venture capital. There are, however, three main paths.

The first path is the least common. Out of college or after two years at a management consulting firm or investment bank, or after graduating from business school, a person is hired as an analyst or associate at a venture capital firm. Sometimes, business school graduates are hired as associates, senior associates or vice presidents. After two to six years, successful associates are invited to become principals or partners. How long it takes to move up depends on your performance and the rate of growth of the venture firm. If the firm is growing quickly, it is often faster and less risky for the firm to promote young associates than to bring in experienced hires.

Commencing on the venture path by first working for a VC-funded start up can be a credible strategy for putting yourself on a venture capitalist's radar.

This second path, to be hired by a VC firm as an experienced professional information technology, health services, or biotech, is more common. After two to six years (normally after attending business school), these hires are invited to become a principal or partner. Finally, successful entrepreneurs may be asked to join a venture firm as a partner in their 30s or 40s. In all cases, once someone is a partner, the percent of the "carry" (profits) they receive increases the longer they stay at the firm and the more important their investments have been to the profitability of the firm.

Job Titles

Disclaimer: *The titles used in venture capital do not necessarily correspond to common investment banking definitions, though they seem to be moving in that direction. To muddy the water a little further, each venture capital firm will apply titles differently. An applicant should pay extra attention to the actual job description in venture capital.*

Analyst/Associate—entry level

If you are coming out of college and have little experience in the working world, this is your starting spot in the world of VC. This position is called associate (or sometimes analyst), depending on the firm. Be aware that most firms do not hire straight out of undergrad (because hands-on experience is such an important component to the business). Display some entrepreneurial activity in your background and some type-A, oddball experience—a pilot's license, racing a sailboat to Bermuda, running an investment club of students, starting a boxer shorts company and so forth. Most importantly, you need to be fun, confident, quantitatively skilled and willing to work hard.

Associate/Senior Associate/Principal/V.P.—partner track

If you have industry experience (e.g., telecommunications, medical devices, consumer products, software) and/or have your MBA, this is the position you're shooting for. This position is often considered "partner track." An MBA is almost always a prerequisite, and a science/engineering undergraduate degree is even more valuable among many firms. The important attributes to show are good judgment, passion, curiosity, a strong ethical barometer and impeccable schmoozing talents.

Junior Partner/General Partner

This position enables you to make investment decisions. It is only conferred on those who have very deep industry experience or those who have shown they can make such decisions at another firm. The good news is that it is not uncommon for serial entrepreneurs and successful industry players to move directly into these positions, after eight to 10 years of professional success in their chosen fields. Venture capital is a business often entered later in one's career. A good set of golf clubs is a prerequisite.

Managing Partner

Raise your own fund and start a venture capital firm! The easiest path to coming on board as a managing partner is to bring along $10 million. Whether this is family money or LPs who would follow you anywhere, you've just bought yourself a partner-level position. Why, you ask? Because at an average management fee of 2 percent, $10 million pays (give or take) your salary. So in effect, the venture firm takes no money away from the GP in order to bring you on board.

Since cash-filled duffel bags no longer hang on trees, figure out your probability of success before you start spending hundreds of hours banging on doors. Look at the numbers. There aren't many positions available, and the ones that exist are hard to find. Why?

- **The venture capital industry is small.** It is made up of only several hundred small firms (each consisting of between two and 40 people). People rarely leave venture capital once they're in. It's too much fun spending money on the latest ideas, working with highly motivated and intelligent people and the latest ideas, and making lots of money. It's also hard for a venture capitalist to transfer into more regimented careers.

- **The old boys' network is in full force in this corner of the economy.** The portion of partners with degrees from Harvard and Stanford is very high (anecdotally, roughly 80 percent Harvard and 15 percent Stanford).
- **The demand for positions is so great that the openings are often filled through networking and are rarely publicly advertised.** In addition, executive search firms like Spencer Stuart (www.spencerstuart.com) should be a tool used during the partnership hunt. They continue to run many partner-level searches for venture firms, although some VCs are hiring HR executives to bring recruiting efforts in-house.

The industry numbers

How big is the venture capital industry? The number changes depending on what you call a "Venture Capital" firm. The National Venture Capital Association estimates about 8,000 VC professionals. We came up with the following estimates for the number of positions nationwide in the industry, about average.

Analysts/Associates (entry level): 750-1,000
Senior Associates/VP (partner track): 1,000-1,500
Partners: 4,000
Firms: 700-750

The most authoritative source for companies of the types listed above is Pratt's Guide to Venture Capital Sources (published by Thomson Financial). You should check it out in the reference section of your local library. However, if you call these firms, you'll find out that a fair number are either gone or winding down. And, some firms aren't listed in Pratt's because they are new and haven't been added yet. Other firms simply don't want to advertise themselves at all. Estimating the senior associate and analyst/associate numbers is difficult because the turnover at these positions is rapid (two to four years). Our educated guess is shown above.

Targeting the Firm You Want

The most prominent and traditional venture firms are located in the San Francisco area and Boston. New York tends to have later stage, lower technology firms with more capital deployed per transaction, and, as a venture capital city, follows closely behind the top two.

Don't overlook the less prominent, less competitive geographic areas with high entrepreneurial growth like Sacramento, North Carolina, New Jersey,

Utah, Colorado, Washington State, Atlanta, and Virginia. The growth of these venture capital communities is not far behind the rise of the entrepreneurs, and you can get in on the ground floor. Other reasons to check these locations out include:

- It might be easier to get a job.
- The day-to-day job is the same or better (because you'll end up having more responsibility).
- Quality of life will be better because of lower pressure, fewer constraints on behavior and lower cost of living.

Don't just target the high-prestige, private funds. Look at university funds, SBICs and venture divisions of corporations. If your ultimate goal is to work for the better known firms, your best bet might be to pursue the lower profile firms, prove yourself for a few years, and then make the move to the big leagues.

On the other hand, working at the most prestigious firms gives you:

- More job opportunities down the road.
- Higher name recognition.
- A better platform from which to meet people in the industries you follow.
- A front row seat on how the best minds in the business think.

Venture Capital Interviews

CHAPTER 5

Getting the Interview

VC firms are inundated with requests for interviews and informational interviews. The time of venture capitalists is precious. If a VC firm lets it be known they have a single summer internship available, they can expect 300 resumes from people at the top 10 business schools. Now that you're more aware of what you are up against, here's a glint of hope—as a whole, venture capital firms are always hiring.

Network, network

So what can you do? Network. Ultimately, networking and schmoozing is the key to a job search in every industry, but it is even more so in the VC industry. Building contacts in the industry is key to finding out about job openings and getting an interview. It helps to have a strong recommendation from someone the VC respects.

The other way to get an interview is to have deep industry experience. This takes a few years, so it's not for the impatient.

Another strategy to up your chances at an interview—do your research. Target a niche attractive to VC firms. Read the trade press or go to a large trade show and catch up on the buzz.

Use your contacts

By far the best way to approach a venture capital firm is via a simple introduction to one of their partners through someone within your professional circle. "Johnny Trustworthy suggested I contact you about ..." will make a big difference. This is no different than the process used by entrepreneurs to get an introduction to VCs. Part of your job should be finding people who are in a position to make this introduction. All VCs work with lots of lawyers, bankers, portfolio companies and boards of directors. Poll your network to see who might know the right people at these outfits, as well as the VC firms themselves.

...and research

Then get access to VentureOne (a Dow Jones product) or VentureXpert (a Thomson Financial product). These databases are very expensive, but you should be able to get access at a local business school or at a friend's investment bank or venture capital firm.

VentureOne and VentureXpert chronicle investments reported by venture capital firms across the U.S. They give you the name of the company invested, which VC firms made the investment, how much was invested, and a short description of what the company does. By studying the information, you may glean an indication of what are currently considered hot investments. You might also start to see patterns where certain names of firms are repeatedly attached to companies that interest you. This info will help you focus your list of preferred venture capital firms.

Hit the web to find out about each of the companies in that space, the VCs that invested in them, and the opinions of journalists who write about the niche. As a low-cost informational supplement on the tech industry and its day to day VC transactions, take a look at CNET News (free at news.com.com), TheDeal (partially free at www.thedeal.com) and Venturewire (some portions are free—www.venturewire.com). Sign up for e-mail postings from both of the latter, to stay up- to- date on events, industry movers and shakers and deal alerts. Develop your own ideas about the market and find other private companies that haven't yet attracted investors. Trade shows are among the best way to research companies. Once you have developed ideas backed up by research, you can approach and impress a VC.

Kauffman Fellowship

Another way to get a post-MBA job in VC is the Kauffman Fellows Program (www.kauffmanfellows.org). Ewing Marion Kauffman created the $1 billion Kauffman Foundation in 1992 to support youth development programs and to accelerate entrepreneurship in America. The fellowship is one of the foundation's innovative programs. Its mission is to increase the number of well-trained venture capitalists in the U.S. by placing and paying top candidates to work as associates in prestigious venture capital firms. It is an excellent program, and has been responsible for a significant percentage of the next generation of venture capitalists over the last few years. Kauffman fellows now represent their own alumni group within the VC industry and use that network to help other alums.

Recruiters specializing in venture capital/private equity:

- Glocap Search—www.glocap.com
- Highland Partners—www.highlandpartners.com
- Pinnacle Group International—www.pinnaclegroup.com
- Phoenix Group International—www.phxgrpintl.com
- Spencer Stuart—www.spencerstuart.com

Websites that post VC job placement ads:

- Vault.com—www.vault.com
- Monster—www.monster.com
- CareerBuilder—www.careerbuilder.com
- Craigs List—www.craigslist.org

Acing the Interview

As mentioned before, VC firms are always looking for people. When a firm finds someone they really like, they can afford to hire them. The simple reason is that the "right" person will add a lot more value than they cost.

So who is the "right" person? As it turns out, the right person for a VC firm can have almost any background—degrees ranging from psychology to English, and industry experience from nonprofit and government to management consulting, investment banking, business operations and of course, entrepreneurial activities. That said, the majority of open positions from associate to partner between 2007 and 2008 called for technical and operational domain (industry) expertise, an MBA from a top five school, a technical undergraduate degree and no less than several years of direct transactional experience as either a VC or M&A investment banker.

A partner's advice

What are venture capital firms typically looking for? Every venture capitalist looks for a unique set of characteristics when evaluating new recruits. Roger Akers, founding partner of Akers Capital, points out that in-depth due diligence experience is crucial for those considering venture capital as their next career move.

"Strong analytical due diligence skills are necessary to evaluate these companies. To articulate the issues at hand facing any startup is also a key point. After all, it will be your responsibility to sell your firm's partners on the merits of the investment you recommend."

He continues, "Individuals trying to enter into the VC world need to be aware of the different aspects of due diligence. In particular, one area that is often lacking but critical is doing a complete market segmentation analysis on companies in one's field of focus. Figure out who the competitors and complimentary players are. What is the best channel/sales strategy? Product pricing structure?" Having a thorough understanding of how to address these questions will help newly-minted venture capitalists to be successful from a marketing and business perspective for their industries of choice.

A strong candidate will have a winning personality, an analytical mind and keen business judgment. VC firms are tiny compared to most other professional outfits. They are high-pressure partnerships where the alchemy of strong personalities becomes critical to the success of the firm. VC candidates often interview with every professional at a firm—and typically, everyone in the firm has veto power.

A straightforward process

On the other hand, VC interviews are not tricky. Generally, there are no brainteasers or case questions. (The only brainteaser asked of an East Coast MBA graduate who is now in the venture capital field was to add up all the numbers from 0 to 100 in his head as quickly as possible.) A VC interview is a chance for venture capitalists to get a sense of you, the same way they do when meeting with entrepreneurs. That's how VCs make investment decisions—by gut instinct. Hiring is no different.

As a result, the interviews are often very personal in nature. You may be asked questions about your family, your friends, your former co-workers and bosses, even your romantic relationships. The VC wants to know if he/she can bear to work closely with you and depend on you for million dollar decisions. Pay attention to your meetings with analysts and associates when interviewing. They are often just as important, if not more so, than the partners.

Corporate VC interviews vary a great deal, depending on the company. While a few corporations may have completely separate funds for doing deals, most are structured as groups, divisions or subsidiaries of the parent company. The interviews for these groups are therefore likely to be similar to most corporate interviews. Be prepared to answer questions about company strategy, investments that should be considered, or new directions and paths to be taken. You should therefore do enough research to understand the corporation's lines of business, current strategic direction and challenges that it faces (now or in the near future). A question that has been asked might sound something like, "If our company decided to sell off one or more of our business lines, which line would you choose?"

Questions in VC interviews typically fall into three categories: questions about your expertise, questions about the VC process and personality/fit questions. Sample questions are listed below.

Sample Expertise Questions

What are the major trends in your industry?

First, be able to explain the big picture. "My industry built overcapacity over the last six years, so a wave of consolidation is beginning." "Explosive growth and competition for technical talent has made the business unprofitable, so we are looking overseas." This shows you can frame market forces in simple and understandable ways.

Second, explain trends that would only be apparent to an observant insider. "There was an assumption in the industry, based on macro price competition, that the customer didn't want higher prices. Turns out consumers believed that higher prices indicated quality, so the companies positioned in the upper tier have fared better." "Four of the six competitors didn't pay close enough attention to the standards bodies and wasted two years building software that won't be compatible with the next generation databases. They're in trouble and they don't even know it yet." This sort of insight shows you get how things really work.

Can you explain why your former company took the path they did?

Here, provide more insight, more demonstration that you "get it." "They said it was a strategic alliance, but in reality, it appears the board of directors chose the path of least resistance."

When you did that project, did you use a certain technology?

What did you think of it? Review all the projects and jobs on your resume. What specific details did you observe and think about during or after the project. How did you make your decisions and why?

Talk about one of your favorite investments.

If you have any work experience in a venture environment (as a VC analyst, corporate business development professional, investment banker or even entrepreneurially-focused attorney), have a good response ready. VCs are interested in hearing a good story, and talking about a past deal gives you the opportunity to demonstrate sound judgment in successfully choosing the best investment prospects, communication skills in making a convincing pitch for the potential business opportunity, and overall understanding of what is needed to make a deal work. Mention any exits (e.g., IPO, M&A) that your prior investments may have had. If you have never made any private equity investments, talk about a public stock that you own.

What companies in your industry might make interesting investments?

This is the end game for VCs. Always have an answer for this question

Sample Process Questions

How would you value an investment?

The idea is to get the best deal possible and still have the entrepreneur take your money and give you a seat on the board. Saying that you would use several methods and then triangulate on a number wouldn't be unreasonable. That number would serve as an anchor around which you would begin discussions with the entrepreneurs.

Begin by putting an upper bound on the valuation by estimating the maximum potential exit valuation for a company and then backing into a number by calculating the maximum price the firm could pay and still get their desired return (after subsequent round dilution). That desired return is typically 40 percent per year, or 10 times the invested capital over a reasonable period, such as five years.

The Discounted Cash Flow (DCF) method can only be used on later stage companies with significant profit history and relatively predictable growth plans. Price earnings multiples from comparable public companies do not work well either, since most early-stage startups have no earnings (and may have little to no revenue). A third and more common way VCs hone in on valuation is to look at comparable private equity investments made by other VCs in similar firms. This leads toward the following if/then decision: If the startup in X field/industry has Y dollars of current revenue with a product in Z stage of development, then it will be valued within a specific, predetermined (by the market), dollar range.

When you evaluate a business plan, what's the most critical element you look for?

The answer is management—the brains behind the operation. A good company is a three-legged stool. One leg is management, a second is market opportunity, and the third is the product or technology. Top management is a must, since a solid team can always deal with and change the business model if necessary. A business or market opportunity must also exist, since at the end of the day, somebody has to sell something to make this all worthwhile. With a seasoned team and viable market, any faulty product or technology can be fixed. That said, too many plans are written around technologies that are more feature than stand-alone product.

Why do you want to work at a venture capital firm?

Do not mention trendiness or money.

Would you want to invest in companies geographically near or far from our offices?

You want to invest near the VC offices to make monitoring and supporting the company easier. You would try to increase returns by giving each invested company more attention and thus an increased chance of succeeding. Early stage investments especially need assistance, and some venture firms turn away any entrepreneur with an office that is more than five miles away from the general partnership's headquarters.

On the other hand, it's worthwhile to search for lower valuations on good companies in faraway regions underserved by competing venture capital firms.

What investment areas do you find interesting?

Do some research on a niche within the investment landscape of the firm. It will take hours of reading in the library, but should give you a differentiated interview and show you are truly interested in venture capital. The VC may disagree with you, but as long as you have good reasons for your opinion, and can show them you can disagree confidently and constructively, you score big.

Do you have any questions for me?

This is your big chance to differentiate and you must have some killer questions to show you're a critical thinker. The best place to start is to ask questions about the near-term evolution of the firm. Other good question topics include:

- Average deal size?
- How investments are sourced (and by whom)?
- Average investment- to- exit horizon (first dollar in to last dollar out)?
- Role with portfolio companies (active vs. passive)?
- Due diligence methodology?
- Appetite for syndication? Leading vs. following?
- Sweet spot for deal fundings (Series A, B, C, or later stage)?
- Don't be afraid to ask the partners their thoughts on interesting investment opportunities.

Learn about firm's portfolio companies and which partner sits on which board. Learn the histories of the companies. You can find out most of this from the web and trade press. It also helps to talk to other VCs. Discover companies the venture capital firm (probably) regrets not investing in. Asking about a missed opportunity shows you know that all firms err—besides showing that you've done your research.

Sample Personality/Fit Questions

What makes a good venture capitalist?

Everyone will have their own favorite answers for this question, but you won't lose any points by talking about curiosity, passion, a desire to be in an entrepreneurial environment, creating value, and learning something new every day. Also, venture capital is a very small club where reputations have little room for a second chance. A strong sense of ethics will serve you well throughout your career.

Charles Harris, chairman and CEO of publicly-held New York venture firm Harris & Harris Group, is a firm believer in life experience as value-added characteristic of any successful VC.

"What makes a successful venture capitalist? Effectiveness, broad life experiences and diverse backgrounds brought to the table. Enough experience to know when you need to bring in some help."

Where do you want to be in five years?

This is a question asked by very few VCs, but you should have an answer prepared nonetheless. If the position you are interviewing for is pre-MBA, express a desire to attend business school and be in a position to work in the venture capital industry somewhere. Many firms are worried about making false promises to young professionals if the person doesn't fit into a partner track position, so they might be more comfortable if you don't say, "I want to be a partner at your firm."

If the position is a partner track position, you probably want to suggest you are looking for a place as a partner in five years, preferably at their firm.

Would you ever want to be an entrepreneur?

If you are a pre-MBA candidate, it's fine to say yes. Most VC types have entrepreneurial leanings and vice versa. However, for a partner-track candidate, this is a dangerous question. If a VC firm is going to give you a coveted partner-track position, it wants you to stay in the firm and make it a lot of money.

What will you do if you don't get a job here or in the venture capital industry?

Say you'd work on leads with other VC firms, or with related businesses like investment banks, market research firms, or small companies that might interest VCs. The keys here are 1) to be excited about other jobs that are similar to the job you are interviewing for, and 2) to have other options. VCs instinctively value something higher if there's competition for them (and that includes you). That said, prioritize venture capital.

What did you like about your old job and why did you leave?

Be sure you know the answer to this. The answer to this question should indicate your strengths and why VC is the right industry for you at this point. Be clear about why you are moving on, but don't complain excessively about your previous job.

What in your life are you most proud of?

Have some great stories prepared from the "personal" section at the bottom of your resume.

What can you do for us that others can't?

There are many ways to ask this question, but the point is clear: "Why are you the best candidate for the job?" Have a good answer, but refrain from sounding arrogant.

CAREERS

ON THE JOB

VENTURE CAPITAL

Training and Responsibilities

CHAPTER 6

Training

Around the industry, one often hears that "venture capital is an apprenticeship business"—it needs to be learned on the job. (That's why there are very few formal training programs at venture capital firms.) A common saying in VC is: "It takes $4 million to make a venture capitalist." This means beginners often start with about $4 million in a series of investments that fail before gaining the insight to make a good investment.

Judgment is the name of the game in the business. No one can define it, but venture capitalists claim they have it and that they know it when they see it in others. "This is a tough job to be qualified for," says Warren Packard. "[A VC's professional life revolves around] judging people and recognizing technology trends."

VC firms pick people who have judgment or have the potential to learn judgment, and let them hang around to get a feeling, a sense, and an awareness, of how to create wealth. That means "training" in a venture firm is limited only by your curiosity and the willingness of the partners to allow access to the deal process.

VC training facilities and programs

No one can be taught to be a venture capitalist. There are programs however, that provide supplementary training in everything from successful due diligence and current term sheet trends, to valuation methodologies.

Domestic

- Atlanta: Venture Capital Institute—facility for VC education (www.vcinstitute.org). Probably one of the better-known training programs in the United States.
- Michigan: U of Michigan B-School, Center for VC and Private Equity Finance (www.umich.edu/~cvpumbs). University-sponsored conferences and seminars on investing and entrepreneurial finance.
- New York: VC Experts—distance learning (www.vcexperts.com). Online and multimedia "how-to" courses on everything from VC fundamentals to the proper structure for forming a new VC partnership.

- National: AltAssets—online private equity information and education (www.altassets.net). Online lectures, case studies and databases filled with information on the business of venture capital.

International

- London: International Faculty of Finance—financial training courses (www.ifftraining.com)
- North and South America, Europe, Asia: Fulcrum Partners—private equity training (www.fulcrum-partners.com)

Job Responsibilities

Associates have three main functions at VC firms: 1) sourcing deals, 2) performing due diligence on potential investments, and 3) supporting the portfolio companies.

Sourcing deals

- Consult with analysts at I-banks or market research firms
- Attend trade shows
- Read trade press releases
- Talk with entrepreneurs
- Probe carefully during due diligence calls
- Gossip with other VCs
- Talk to accountants and lawyers
- Surf the internet for research
- Think strategically/brainstorm about potential opportunities
- Attend investment conferences where companies seeking capital present to an audience of investors
- Build a strong network of ongoing qualified deal flow.

Performing due diligence on potential investments

- Talk to customers
- Research and talk to the competition
- Find and interview industry experts about the market/competition/trends
- Bring in technical consultants to evaluate the technology

- Perform management background checks
- Bring in lawyers to review contracts/patents/licenses etc.
- Bring in accounting consultants to verify financials (or roll up your own sleeves)
- Talk with previous investors
- Spend time with management and at the company looking for red flags

Supporting portfolio companies

- Research and strategic planning
- Attend board of directors meetings
- Help locate and screen potential additions to a company's management team
- Convince new recruits that they should work with your portfolio company
- Support the management team (can be anything from being a friend to "handholding")
- Negotiate and work with I-bankers
- Negotiate and work with acquirers of the company
- Raise more money from other equity sources
- Negotiate with banks for debt financing
- Report to the rest of your VC firm on changes, problems and triumphs
- Help acquire other companies

As an associate, your primary duty will be to support the partners and leverage their time. Remember, they have hired you so they can deploy more money in profitable investments. For the privilege of the apprenticeship, you are expected to create a lot more value for the firm than your compensation would suggest.

Early stage—deal sourcing

In an early stage venture firm, you will be expected to source deals. You need to reach out into the world and bring investment opportunities to the firm. This amounts to calling and visiting companies to ascertain their attractiveness and interest in raising capital. This isn't as easy as it sounds! Deal sourcers will go to trade shows, talk with their networks of friends, read the trade press, work with other VCs, attend local networking events and investment conferences, read unsolicited business plans, and talk to portfolio company managers. There are hundreds of deal sourcers at work at any given time—and being the first VC to a company matters.

When sourcing deals, schmoozing is key. Any acquaintance or friend might give you the next lead on a company. VC associates must build personal relationships with business partners to up the level of trust and interdependence.

Late stage—due diligence

Associates support partners in due diligence analysis of an investment opportunity. Later stage companies are normally no secret (they're typically large enough to have attracted press and other attention). The trick is not to uncover the investment opportunity, but to get a company to take your money. Consequently, the partner is usually the one to source later stage deals. Associates perform due diligence: building spreadsheets and running sensitivity analyses, calling references, investigating competitors, validating legal contracts, visiting remote locations, coordinating with other investors and so on.

Ultimately, associates and partners must decide how best to use the most precious resource: time. Which markets to research? Which company to work on? Which entrepreneur to call back? Which spreadsheet model to build? Which references to call? Which trip to take, which meeting to make? As an apprentice venture capitalist, associates must make decisions all day long. Many of those decisions have to do with which potential assignments to pursue. A venture firm is responsible for the money in its fund, and the clock is ticking.

Investment timeline

If you do your job well, you can look forward to a long and exciting private equity career filled with challenges and rewards. Investing in private companies should never be easy. When done right, however, a successful deal might look something like the following timeline (depicting the life of a startup from seed funding through liquidity). Although the name and dates have been changed to preserve confidentiality, the company is real and its history true. This deal really happened.

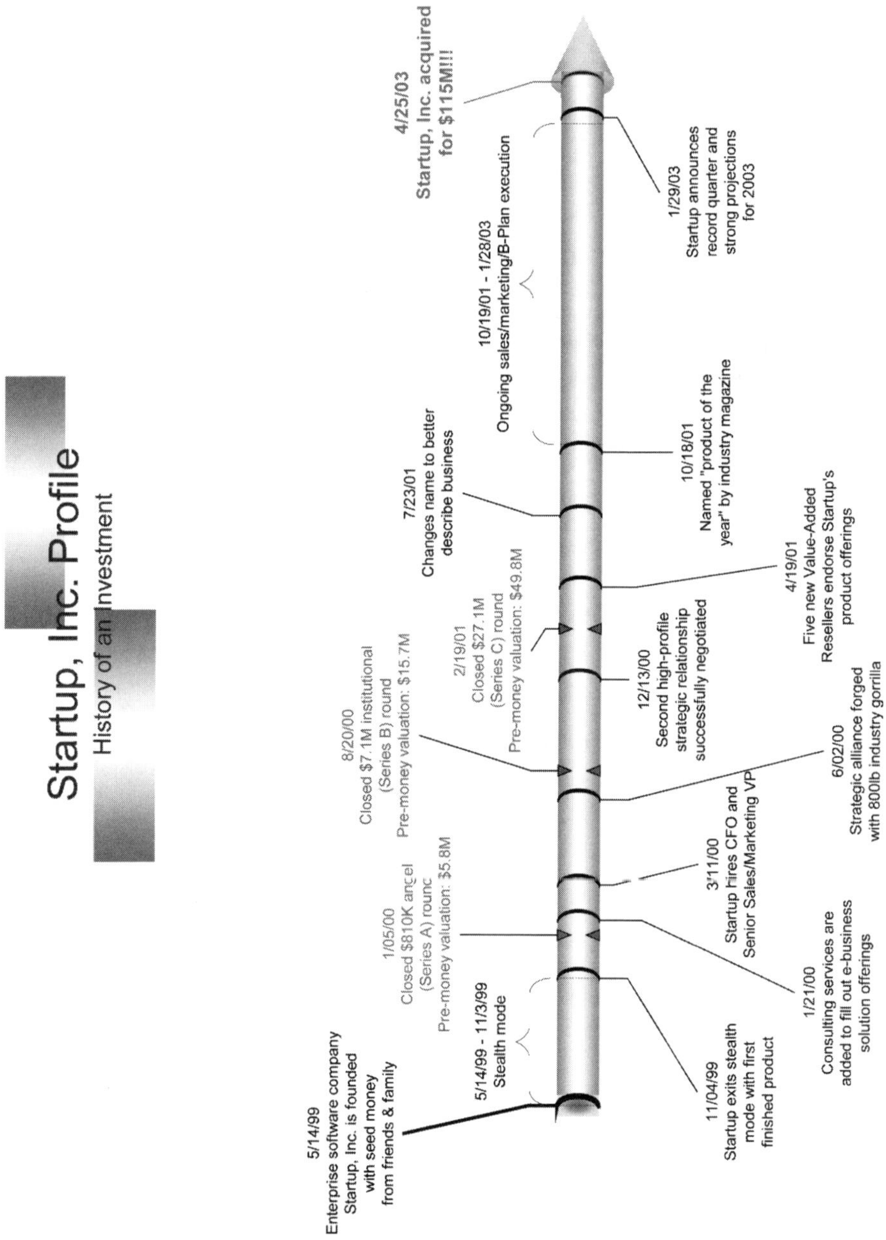

VC Concepts

CHAPTER 7

Among the most significant concepts for venture capital professionals are the capitalization table and the term sheet. This chapter walks you through both of these fundamentals, and also lays out the standard themes part of any due diligence checklist.

Capitalization (cap) table

The cap table breaks down the capitalization structure of the startup, showing individual ownership, share price per round, and more. Cap table formats are as different and numerous as the startups that put them together. Take a look at the table at the end of the book for Startup, Inc., and become familiar with the content (which should be present regardless of the format used). The red flags to focus on in this particular table include:

Management incentive

If the numbers are crunched, you'll notice that the CEO owns about 6.5% of the company (post money). Half of her shares are not yet vested, with the majority of ownership residing in the option pool (which also vests over time). More diligence is required to better understand the option vesting schedule. However, it looks as though the CEO has adequate incentive to perform, while still being "locked in" (incentive not to leave) by the vesting schedule.

On the other hand, the VP of Marketing has an insignificant level of ownership (approximately 0.1%), and is therefore a flight risk. If investors and management believe the Sales and Marketing VP to be irreplaceable, then more options must come his way.

Option pool

Options go hand in hand with management performance incentives, but often also play a very important role in non-managerial employee compensation. In this example, the pool of available options is very low at 3.1%. On average, 15 to 20% is the range to shoot for. Variables in deciding the right pool size include the number of C-level staff that have yet to be hired, as well as projected option requirements for all employees over the course of the current funding being burned through.

When calculating pre-money valuations, pay close attention to the option pool requirements. Any increase in the number of available options needs to happen before a share value can be assigned, as this increase will lower (or dilute) the overall price per share. You will hear the term "fully diluted" often, when discussing valuations and cap tables.

Burn rate

Although the detailed financials will disclose much more about the cash burn rate than the cap table, it is clear that this startup has very high cash needs. The company has raised progressively larger amounts of cash three times over the course of 13 months. This could be a signal for darker days ahead.

Investors

It is a telling sign to see a complete absence of any new investors in a current round of financing. There is some truth to the saying, "If you look around a poker table and cannot spot the sucker, then you're probably it." Stop and ask yourself why no other new investors are interested in the deal. Startup, Inc. fortunately has at least two new investors in every subsequent round.

For strategic investors

Be aware of any other strategic investors/partners that the startup may have, as this can have direct consequences on the future direction and strategy of the startup and its technology.

Also, pay attention to both series (A, B, and C) and class (Common and Preferred) ownership stakes. Who can outvote whom? When? This is where term sheet negotiation will play an important role, since corporate investment objectives are not always aligned with pureplay venture capitalists.

In our example, the strategic investor owns just under 7% of the company, and 19% of the Series C Preferred shares. Since this corporate investor can be outvoted either way, this company will likely negotiate for particular "protective provisions" (see the term sheet in the appendix) that mitigate some of the inherent risks.

Term sheet

The term sheet is normally penned by the lead investor, outlining the terms of investment. The document lays out the amount of an investment and the conditions under which the investors expect the startup to work using VC money.

Why is it necessary? The term sheet is the first step in formalizing the proposed transaction. It serves a practical purpose in initiating "a meeting of the minds" on vital deal points (starting with valuation), reflecting both investors' and startup's essential expectations.

(See glossary and the sample term sheet in the appendix at the back of the book for more detail.)

CONCERNS ADDRESSED BY THE TERM SHEET

VC Perspective	Concerns for investors and startups
• Startup's current/projected valuation • Level of risk associated with investment • Fund's investment objectives and criteria • Projected levels of ROI • Investment liquidity and exit strategies in the event of business distress or failure (downside protection) • Protection of the firm's ability to participate in future rounds if startup meets or exceeds projections (upside protection) • Influence and control over management strategy and decisions • Registration rights in the event of an IPO	• Retention of key members of management team and recruitment of key missing links • Resolution of any conflicts within the investment syndicate • Financial strength of the startup (post-investment) • Tax ramification of proposed investment

Note: From a Netpreneur presentation by Andrew J. Sherman, ESQ

Due diligence checklist

How do you spot a good investment?

If this could be definitively answered, venture capital would be a secure business indeed! Multiple VC firms rejected many of today's most successful companies. And many companies that have received $10 million, $40 million, and even $400 million in venture capital money have disappeared (remember Webvan?).

The "perfect investment" has:

1. A complete management team who you enjoy spending time with. They are loved by their employees, have experience and integrity, and are respected by the investment community.
2. A clearly defined, large and unexploited market opportunity.
3. A finished product that works and addresses a clear market need.
4. A set of customers with money to spend, and the ability and desire to spend it.
5. A company that is located in a place where it is easily monitored.
6. A low price.
7. No other institutional investors, or excellent early stage investors.
8. A leading position in the targeted market.
9. A unique set of capabilities that will keep the company ahead of the competition, with or without patents (otherwise known as barriers to entry).

All other opportunities are "hairy," displaying some element of risk. But what doesn't?

Basic due diligence questionnaire and checklist

Every venture firm has its own operating procedures and ideas for what diligence items to focus on the most. Nevertheless, the due diligence themes below tend to set the standard:

1. The opportunity

I. Is there a market niche and reason for investment?

A. A strategic investor should ask:

1. Why is this candidate relevant?
2. Is there support from the business unit?
3. Where within our company is the candidate's business/product important?
4. What does the startup company want from us?
5. What is the strategic rationale?
    a. Define/Quantify Success
    b. How strategic is the deal/importance of investment (scale of 1-10)?

B. Financial investor

1. Top-down space identification
    a. Focus on next "hot" space/problem to solve
    b. Center in on best companies in space
2. Bottom up
    a. Search for strong businesses, model, and management teams, regardless of space

II. Overall market size—Is this a billion dollar market?

III. Customers

A. Value to potential (visible) customers (quantifiable annual dollar amt)

1. Who are (or will be) the investee's customers?
2. Is there a demand/pain in the market?
    a. Do potential customers currently need what investee is offering?
    b. Will investee's product/solution directly (and positively) affect their customer's business/bottom line?

IV. Ability to leverage from first customer

A. Customer phone calls

1. History with investee company and how customer is using their products?
2. Experience with investee's management team?
3. Where does customer see the value in investee's product/solution?

4. Is customer actively using the product, or is this still a trial period? Is there money changing hands (revenue)?
5. Alternatives customer may be considering (instead of investee).
6. Risks/hurdles/main concerns going forward.

2. Valuation/Financials/Funding/Resources/Capitalization

I. Value compared to the industry and market

A. Bridge company valuation from last round: how does increase in value compare to the improvement in their business from last round?

B Multiples (Revenue, Headcount, Profitability)

C. Similar recent transactions in private and public markets

D. Have milestones from prior round been reached? (How far has the company come since the last round)

II. Size of round?

A. Use of funds

B. Will current round of funding last through profitability or liquidity event?

C. Is the available option pool large enough to last through next round/liquidity event?

1. If not, investee should increase pool, and calculate additional options in cap table (this is included in calculating a fully diluted valuation).

III. Size of our investment?

IV. Amount lead is investing?

V. Marketing costs?

VI. Margin / Profitability

A. What is the planned path to profitability? Time period through breakeven?

VII. Who are the key (prior and current) investors. Who is the lead in this round?

A. Are prior investors committing to pro rata investment for current round?

B. Syndicate/investor phone calls

1. Background checks on portfolio (on lead); track record?
2. What is their history with the investee?
3. Knowledge of management team?
4. Where is the perceived value in this investment?

5. Comfort with valuation?
6. Risks/hurdles/main concerns going forward?

VIII. What is the burn rate, cash on hand, and monthly revenue run rate?

A. What is the current # of employees vs. projected for next 12 months?

IX. Clear exit strategy and timing:

A. IPO vs purchase by us (if corporate vc) vs. purchase by someone else

3. Sustainable advantage

I. Is there a clear advantage vs. alternatives?

A. Management team
B. Unique IP (intellectual property)- patents, etc.
C. First mover/branding
D. Product
   1. Ease of use/utility
   2. Technology assessment

II. Is the preemption/domination of market possible?

III. What other barriers to entry has the company erected?

A. Exclusive licenses (spectrum, region of the country, etc.)
B. Partnerships/agreements with vendors, distributors, etc.
   1. Exclusivity?
C. First mover/large head start
D. Ease of use, etc.

IV. Showstoppers—Is there a deal-breaker?

4. Competitors

I. What serious/entrenched competitors have been looked at?

II. Who in this space would we consider if we decide not to invest in this candidate?

III. Exposure to ambush/risk of being overtaken?

IV. Is there competency that competitors lack?

V. Does the company have a speed advantage?

VI. Competitors' ability to replicate vs. competitors as partners?

VII. Where in product cycle vs. investee?

VIII. Resources/support (investors, profitability, etc.)

5. Market entry

I. Is there a viable entry strategy?

A. Low hanging fruit?

II. Punchy/compelling story

A. Experienced/charismatic CEO (great salesperson)

B. Strong/experienced VP BizDev/Sales

C. Ability to create hype

III. Direct vs. channel distribution?

6. Management and their ability to execute

I. Biographies on principals

A. Management experience/track record

1. Ability to execute and scale business plan

II. Relationships

A. Do we know the management team? Have they been recommended?

B. Can mgmt be trusted (Integrity)? Are background checks necessary?

III. Strategic investor: Who from our firm has already met with the company's management team (Engineering team, etc.)? Comments?

A. What other groups from within our company have relationships with investee?

IV. Is there a high-profile management team or CEO?

V. What is their time to market/launch?

VII. What share of the company (including options) does management own?

A. Is management locked in or completely vested? If vested, may need to re-vest options to keep mgmt around for a few years.

VIII. Are there managerial holes to be filled (VP Sales/BizDev, etc.)?

IX. Has management achieved all milestones set during the prior round?

7. Necessity for a fully-baked round:

I. Strategic investor:

A. Standard investment docs, term sheet and financial VC lead (if strategic investor)

B. Any co-investors that are necessary, or conversely, will not allow (if strategic investor)?

II. IP (Intellectual property)—Confirmation that investment candidate is the sole owner of all IP.

III. Solid board (Relationships, etc.)

A. During which investment round did each board member join? What is their percentage of ownership?

8. Risks:

I. Business

II. Financial

III. Management

IV. Legal

V. Product

VI. Market

VII. Industry

Compensation and Lifestyle

CHAPTER 8

Pay and Perks

Venture capital firms offer unique types of compensation. They are:

Closing Bonus: A bonus is often given to lower-level employees for sourcing or doing due diligence when an investment is closed. Most early stage firms do not give this lower-level bonus, although some, like Summitt Partners and Battery Ventures, do. This bonus is intended to focus their attention on the best deals and work hard to get them closed.

Co-investment: This common perk allows VCs to invest their own money alongside the firm in some deals. If a firm is successful, the upside of co-investment can far exceed salary and bonuses.

Carry: A percentage of the profits the firm makes. Carry is the Holy Grail of venture capital. A senior associate might get 0.25 to 0.5 percent initially. A Partner might start with 0.5 percent and move to 4 percent over his/her career. Example: if a firm has a $100 million fund and triples it over 8 years, profit might be $200 million. A 1 percent carry would thus be worth $2 million dollars.

The following are very general salary figures for the venture capital industry:

- Analyst:

  Salary $45,000—$70,000.
  Annual Bonus $15,000.
  Closing Bonus, Yes.
  Co-investment, No.

- Associate:

  Salary $80,000—$120,000.
  Annual Bonus $50,000.
  Closing Bonus, Yes. Co-investment, Yes.
  Carry, sometimes a small amount.

- Sr. Associate/Principal/VP:

  Salary $150,000.
  Bonus $150,000.
  Closing Bonus, Yes.
  Co-investment, Yes.
  Carry, probably.

- Partner:

  Salary $200,000—$300,000.
  Annual Bonus $500,000.
  Closing Bonus, No.
  Co-investment, Yes.
  Carry, Yes.

Uppers and Downers

Uppers

1. There is a reason that very few people ever willingly leave their VC careers. Where else can you have so much fun investing other people's money (plus some of your own), while being "in the middle of it all"?

2. You often get to be the one making decisions because you have money.

3. Over the long term, financial security will cease to be an issue, because the job is well paying and you should eventually get "carry" or equity in the firm.

4. You have access to the best minds—the people you work with are typically some of the smartest and most interesting. Successful venture capitalists have interests and hobbies as diverse as mountain climbing to playing jazz in nightclubs.

5. Your job is to absorb and enjoy the positive creative energy of entrepreneurs and direct it toward successful execution.

6. You could suddenly become rich if one of your companies does extremely well and you were able to co-invest or you have carry.

7. You have access to the best information systems.

Downners

Because so many think of the venture capital industry as "the hot job to have," people often forget to question whether it is the right job for them. Here is a list of some of the negatives we hear from those who have worked in the industry for a while.

1. Unless you work with a hands-on early-stage VC firm known for taking an active role in building successful companies, you don't have pride of ownership in anything. You're just an investor, not a builder.
2. VC is a slow path to wealth compared with the immediate cash income you get in investment banking, hedge funds or even management consulting.
3. It can be argued that venture capital is fundamentally a negative process. Because you reject 99 of every 100 plans, year after year, over time you focus on figuring out what is wrong with a company. You can then reject it and get on to the next deal. What is wrong with the management? The technology? The deal terms? The strategy? If you tend to have a contrarian disposition, after just a few years, that mentality may bleed into your life. What is wrong with my partners? What is wrong with my spouse? What is wrong with me? Oh, the angst! If this reaction hits too close to home, venture capital might not be for you. What fun is it to search through hundreds and thousands of business plans and ideas for that one rare gem, if you aren't an eternal optimist?
4. Because you reject 99 of every 100 entrepreneurs, you can make some enemies, no matter how nice and helpful you try to be. No one likes rejection, and passionate entrepreneurs have long memories.

Lifestyle

Hours

Venture capitalists typically work at least 60 to 70 hours per week. (More on average on the East Coast over West, and in general partnerships over corporate venture groups. It takes a lot of effort to keep your edge.) The VC community is still a small one. Networking and having the informational edge are vital to VC career success. All of this takes time, especially at the beginning of your career when you're just building a reputation. That said, if you enjoy what you are doing, much of it will not feel like work.

Dress

Increasingly, venture capitalists are opting for business casual garb (particularly on the West Coast)*. For one, VCs don't need to dress to impress—they're the ones with the money. Venture capitalists also work extensively with high-tech entrepreneurs, who are normally casually dressed (to say the least). You'll see a surprising number of Timex watches. (Of course, this casual dress does not always hold true, particularly on the East Coast, where Wall Street judges one's "rank" by the cost of one's suit.)

Diversity

Diversity is a serious issue to the venture community. There are still very few women and hardly any African-Americans in the industry (as the founder and managing partner of Venture Strategy Partners, Joanna Gallanter is one of the few in the expanding contingent of women leaders helping to shape the VC business). It's always hard to say why one industry moves more quickly or slowly in this regard than another, but it seems venture capital has moved slowly because of the confidence issue. For everyone in this wealth creation chain—the entrepreneur, the VC, the investment bank, the press—guessing which companies will succeed is very difficult and picking wrong has a serious impact on the bottom line. As a default, most people move to a mode of "pattern recognition." If they see a management team, business model or market position they have made money with before, they tend to choose it. In spite of everything, race and gender are factors that people "pattern recognize" as well. In a high-risk business, white men look safer—unfair though this may be.

Many venture firms have been trying to address the issue of diversity. In the end, if you are a woman or an ethnic minority, you need to do what everyone else needs to do: become an expert in an industry, show good judgment, and schmooze.

A Day in the Life of a Venture Capital Analyst

6:00 a.m.: Wake up. Check BlackBerry messages for any developments overnight. Then log on the computer to read business headlines, scanning web sites such as The Wall Street Journal, The New York Times Dealbook blog and Yahoo finance. Download the latest podcast from web sites like Venture Voice or Venture Capital Update to listen to on the way in.

7:00 a.m.: Arrive in the office and begin replying to e-mails. Then take a more in-depth read of financial news, paying specific attention to major publications like The Wall Street Journal and Financial Times. Also read various trade publications, both online and in print, that covers your specific area of coverage. Take notes of new ideas and companies that might be a good candidate for a capital infusion.

8:00 a.m.: With names of people and companies culled from the morning's research, use the internet to research information and contact details on them. Check your firm's internal database to see if someone else on your team has contacted the companies. Create files for the ones that hold potential, send yourself an e-mail as a reminder to call them during business hours.

9:00 a.m.: Respond to e-mails and voice mails from the day before. People you are communicating with are primarily entrepreneurs, other VCs, and personal acquaintances.

9:30 a.m.: Attend morning staff meeting with the general partner assigned to your area. Here you'll give a quick run down on some interesting stories in the news that might impact the sector you cover. Also, this is an opportunity to gauge the general partner's interest by providing the names of a few ideas or companies that might be looking for funding.

10:00 a.m.: You attend a meeting with a group of entrepreneurs who want to make their pitch. You read the business plan for five minutes. One general partner sits in with you. The other GP, who planned to be there, cannot make it because he has a conference call with a portfolio company facing some challenges. You sit politely through the presentation, and identify the three critical issues facing the company. During the question and answer phase, you think of how to politely extract more information about those three issues, all the while evaluating whether you would want to work with this team or not.

In the end, you decide to make some calls to gather more information about the market, or a competitor, but you feel that there's a very low probability you would ever invest. You wish you could just kill the deal, but the management team is reasonable (though not great), the customer need they have identified may actually exist (you don't know first-hand, so you will need to call around), and you may learn something by taking it to the next step. Plus, in the back of your mind, you know the market for good deals is very competitive, and you don't want to reject a deal too quickly.

11:00 a.m.: Phone the people who called during your meeting. These people include entrepreneurs, analysts, other VC's, and your lunch appointment. You find out from another VC that the company you almost invested in two months ago just got funded by a competing firm. You wonder if you made a mistake. You find out from an entrepreneur you were hoping to back that he wants his son to be a co-founder and owner of the firm. You abandon all hope. You learn from an analyst that AT&T has decided to stop its trial of a new technology because it doesn't work, which creates an opportunity for companies with an alternative solution. You happen to know about two small companies, one in Boston and one in Denver, which have alternative solutions. You make a note to yourself to call them to get a status report.

12:30 p.m.: Lunch with a small business you had reached out to a few months ago about their interest in receiving some venture capital. The company has already shopped their idea to a few other firms, and you're hoping to gauge their interest and hopefully woo them. This would be the final step before you arrange a meeting between the company and your VC firm's general partners. Bringing in a hot new client is a major coup for any analyst—and they're interested.

2:00 p.m.: Get back into the office and write up a report on the new company you just had lunch with, including all the relevant information, how much funding they are looking for and your analysis of the company's potential. Much of this legwork would have likely been done already as you built your relationship with this company. Once the report is complete, you forward it to the general partner and arrange a time for the company to come into the office.

3:00 p.m.: You and a partner meet with a portfolio company on a conference call. This is a company you helped bring to the firm and know well. Unfortunately, it is facing some challenges and you offer to screen executive recruiters to help find a new CFO for it. The GP offers to talk to two M&A firms to get a first opinion about what might be done to sell the company over the next six months. At the end of the call, the GP gives you three names and numbers of recruiters, which you add to your own contacts.

4:30 p.m.: You make due diligence calls for a potential investment you have been following for two months. Last week you called the company's customers, and they seemed happy for the most part. Today, you are calling the personal references of the management team. The idea is to get as much negative information as possible. You need to discover any potential character or personality flaws any member of the team may have. VC firms are "due diligence machines," doing the hard work of making sure a company is what it says it is.

5:00 p.m.: A conference call is scheduled with a company that your boss has asked you to do research on. After about 30 minutes on the call, you've determined that it does not fill the criteria your firm is looking for. However, once the CEO has explained his business plan, you begin to ask about competitors. During the course of the conversation, you find out about other companies that might fit the firm's criteria and have broadened your knowledge about the sector you cover.

5:30 p.m.: You make calls to the West Coast. You also check your stocks and confirm dinner plans. You do some miscellaneous surfing on the web to gather some articles about the technology areas you cover.

7:00 p.m.: Dinner with two other young VCs downtown. You talk mostly about life, sports, travel and relationships, but also about the latest deals, cool business ideas, and recent successes. You find out that a competing firm just made 30 times their money on a deal you never saw. You also find out that a company you turned down which was invested in by someone else is about to go bankrupt. A train missed; a bullet dodged.

A Day in the Life of a Venture Capital General Partner

6:00 a.m.: Immediately log on to your BlackBerry to sift through whatever e-mails have come in overnight. While doing so, you multi-task between getting yourself ready for a day of work and scanning through headlines on everything from blogs to major newspapers. What catches your attention are any venture capital related stories, or articles on your portfolio companies, their competitors or industry.

7:00 a.m.: Being based in the Silicon Valley, you dial into a 7 a.m. board meeting for a New York-based company that is in your portfolio. You also serve as a director on the board. The company is looking for another stage of financing to help expand, but the business plan has not advanced to the point which you would have liked it. Worried that this company might not reap the kind of rewards first envisioned, you suggest bringing on a co-lead investor to spread the risk. That doesn't go over well with the board, but they send the idea to a special finance committee and give you some time to work out a plan.

8:30 a.m.: On the way into work, you roll telephone calls to various angel investors that might want to come in on the deal. You also use this time to check your voicemail before arriving into work, and dispatch analysts and other members of the firm to begin working on various projects.

9:00 a.m. Arrive at work, and begin responding to voicemails as you dial into another conference call, which you quickly put on speaker phone so that it gives you a bit more mobility in the office. The CEO of a portfolio company gives you an update on profit margins and new products, while at the same time you pore over your e-mail. A note pops into your in-box from the CEO of the company you had a board meeting with earlier in the morning: the finance committee has approved the proposal for a co-investor. You send out a few more e-mails to the angels telling them that the deal is a go, hoping one of them will bite. Another e-mail is from a venture capital fund that wants help on a deal they are working on, and another one catches your eye from a hot internet company you've been reading about.

10:00 a.m.: You attend a meeting of all the general partners at the venture capital firm to go over what was discussed in meetings held earlier in the morning with analysts. There are reports about new companies that might be good to take meetings with. Another general partner talks about how a rival VC firm muscled in on a deal, and is asking for ideas about how to sweeten your firm's own offer without causing any excess risk. Your forte has always been about spotting new talent, so a long session of crunching numbers isn't exactly the way you wanted to spend the morning. But it also shows how much you can learn before 10 a.m., and what keeps the world of venture capital exciting.

11:30 a.m.: An analyst that reports to you holds a quick meeting to discuss early stage funding for a company that has so far shown some promising work. The analyst has completed most of the due diligence and wants to set up a meeting, but you feel it might be a bit premature. You've got a working lunch set up for noon, and crunched for time, you tell him to come back to you later in the week with some more details.

12:00 p.m.: Two CEOs from companies in the firm's portfolio agree to meet with you for lunch. You've had an idea for a while that both companies might want to share technology, maybe even team up on new products together. These two upstart companies have very similar cultures, and could make a blockbuster team if they cooperated. The CEOs seem hesitant that you're trying to merge the two together, which wouldn't be such a bad idea in your mind. They agree to explore some opportunities, and you give them some direction about how to go about it. With work out of the way, you spend the balance of the lunch talking about current events, film and updates about your personal lives.

2:00 p.m.: Rushing back into the office after lunch, you do the all too familiar check of e-mail and voicemail. The good news is that one of the angels confirmed they'll provide the funding needed for the New York-based company you had a conference call with in the morning. The bad news is that an offer to acquire a company owned by another venture capital firm was turned down. The deal would have been a perfect fit for the company run by the CEO you just had lunch with. But, perhaps that gives your lunch partners even more incentive to work together.

3:00 p.m.: You meet with a candidate to become CFO of one of the portfolio companies that you manage. This is among the best parts of the job because you get to meet new people, and hear their ideas about how to make one of your companies great. During some interviews you use the lulls to map out strategy for other ideas you have. But, this one in particular is interesting—and the candidate seems to be simply perfect for the job. He's also turning out to be an expert in an area where you see some opportunity to make more deals, and could even be a potential CEO sometime down the line.

4:00 p.m.: The chief counsel from the portfolio company looking for more funding calls to go over a proposed term sheet. The phone call was last minute, and mostly informational, as you haven't lined up all the specifics yet from the angel. You assure the lawyer that the angel will agree to the deal terms, but you're privately not sure.

4:30 p.m.: With some downtime before the next meeting, you again scan over the financial headlines, sift through some e-mails, and make a few personal calls. There's a stack of due diligence reports about potential deals that seems to be piled high in the corner of your office, but you decide to put it off after a day packed full of conference calls. Perhaps some light reading on the weekend.

5:00 p.m.: The last meeting of the day could hold the most potential. The CEO of a tech company looking to score some financing presents his pitch to you, a few other general partners and analysts. The presentation wasn't the slickest you've seen, but there's no mistaking the facts. Profit margins are strong, new products are in the pipeline, and the company is already becoming somewhat of a darling in Silicon Valley media. There seems to be no hesitance in the eyes of anyone in the room.

6:00 p.m.: On the way home from the office, your BlackBerry beeps. It is from the angel investor you've been trying to get an agreement with all day. It has decided to pull out of the deal. And, with California three hours ahead of time, you use the balance of the evening scrambling to find another angel. You realize that old adage "win some, lose some" applies here, but also know you won more during the day than you lost.

CAREERS

TOP VENTURE CAPITAL FIRMS

VENTURE CAPITAL

3i Group

91 Waterloo Road
London, SE1 8XP UK
www.3i.com

The Scoop

From its humble beginnings in London in 1945, 3i has become an international giant. Spanning three continents with 750 employees in 29 offices, the firm has 25 locations in Europe, as well as two offices each in the U.S and Asia. Listed on the London Stock Exchange under ticker symbol III, 3i became part of the FTSE 100 in 1994.

3i focuses on three specific areas of investment: buy-outs, growth capital, and venture capital.

Investment Strategy

3i's most valuable investments have been in companies in the service and utility sectors. The firm's secondary focus is on consumer goods and industrials. The preferred investment type has been buy-outs, which have been the most profitable type of investments in 3i's portfolio.

Accel Partners

428 University Avenue
Palo Alto, CA 94301
www.accel.com

The Scoop

Founded in 1983, Accel focuses on maverick technology companies. Using what they call a "prepared mind" approach, the firm prides itself on knowledge, experience and connections in the field. Among the first firms to have foresight about the eventual power of the Internet, Accel provided financing for UUNET Technologies in 1993, one of the first venture capital investments in the Internet. Accel was also the first venture capital firm to have its own web site.

Accel continues to have faith in the telecommunications and technology market. Today, Accel manages $3 billion in assets and their portfolio companies that have gone public have generated $100 billion.

Investment Strategy

Accel dedicates all its resources to investment in two sectors: networking and software. This specialization has allowed them to become experts, streamlining their ability to find companies worthy of expenditure. With a rich network composed of companies, executives and experts in these two fields, Accel can quickly recognize the validity of a company or an entrepreneur and make an informed investment decision.

Advanced Technology Ventures

1000 Winter Street, Suite 3700
Waltham, MA 02451
www.atvcapital.com

The Scoop

Advanced Technology Ventures (ATV) has been in business for more than 20 years. With operations on the two coasts in Massachusetts and California, ATV now manages $1.4 billion in capital. The company concentrates in several markets in the technology sector, including healthcare technology, and raises capital for both private and public companies.

In addition to sector-focused investments, the firm specializes in raising a company's standing through effective management. ATV draws on the management experience of its six partners who have either started their own businesses or served as CEOs.

Investment Strategy

ATV's investments have concentrated in North America, with a secondary emphasis in Europe and Israel. The firm's major investments have been in the following four areas: IT infrastructure, software and services, and healthcare.

Alta Partners

One Embarcadero Center, Suite 4050
San Francisco, CA 94111
www.altapartners.com

The Scoop

In 1996, four senior partners from Burr, Egan, Deleage & Co. (BEDCO) pooled their expertise in life sciences, information technology and communications and set up their own firm, Alta Partners. They have since funded 120 companies.

Alta Partners has developed seven venture funds: four focusing on life science and breakthrough technologies; and three funds that invest in the later-stages of private companies and in smaller, undercapitalized public companies. Collectively these funds give Alta Partners $1.5 billion in capital.

Investment Strategy

Alta Partners tends to invest in companies in the fields with which they are most familiar: life science and information technology. They look for companies that provide a one-of-a-kind product and have a large market opportunity. Alta Partners also prefers to be the lead investor for a company, thus earning the firm a seat on the board of directors.

Apax Partners

445 Park Avenue, 11th Floor
New York, NY 10022
www.apax.com

The Scoop

Now the largest venture capital firm in Europe, Apax Partners has over the last 32 years opened offices across Europe, the U.S. and Israel. In its history, Apex has invested in 500 companies worldwide and generated or advised on $12 billion. The firm focuses on seven different sectors: IT, media, healthcare, retail and consumer, financial services and telecommunication.

Investment Strategy

Apax functions in two realms of investment: early-stage companies, and buy-out companies. With the early-stage companies, Apax measures the exclusivity of the product, as well as the size of their possible market, always with the goal of expanding the company into the international arena. With buy-outs, the goal is to achieve rapid growth and conquer new markets.

Atlas Venture

890 Winter Street, Suite 320
Waltham, MA 02451
www.atlasventure.com

The Scoop

Atlas Venture was started in 1980 as part of ING Bank, in the Netherlands. After opening an office in Boston in 1986 Atlas became independent from the bank, ultimately opening offices in Munich, Paris and London. The firm has a specialization in three sectors: communications, life science and information technology.

Atlas Ventures has $2.1 billion in capital and has aided in the launch and development of more than 300 companies.

Investment Strategy

The firm forms strong ties with the companies in which they invest. Atlas Ventures usually monitors the companies closely through membership on their Board of Directors. From this vantage point, Atlas provides assistance to the company in areas such as recruitment, marketing, legal and finance.

Austin Ventures

300 West 6th St., #2300
Austin, TX 78701
www.austinventures.com

The Scoop

Austin Ventures was formed in 1979. Named for the city where it was founded, the firm is dedicated to cultivating local businesses: two-thirds of Austin`s investments are in Texas companies. The result is a strong and integrated local network of entrepreneurs and executives. Austin Ventures may be focused on local projects, but it has national clout with $2.4 billion under management. The firm concentrates in the technology sectors of software, hardware and service and information.

Investment Strategy

Austin defines four categories for their investments. The smallest investment level is internal incubation, for companies that have a history or connection with the firm's members. The money given is $100,000 or less, based on a determination reached through investigation by Austin's practice group. The second level of investment includes levels from $500,00 to $10 million. This amount is for starting up companies and for the first level of fundraising. For companies that already reached the early stage and are looking for expansion, Austin provides $25 to $50 million. Finally, there are special situations such as buy-outs or recapitalization, where the investment level varies widely.

Benchmark Capital

2480 Sand Hill Road, Suite 200
Menlo Park, CA 94025
www.benchmark.com

The Scoop

Benchmark Capital was founded in 1995. In the short time since its founding, in 1995, Benchmark Capital has opened practices in Europe and Israel, in addition to their office in Silicon Valley. Although the three offices work for common goals and specialize in the same area, each functions independently, making investment decisions about businesses in their respective geographic locations.

The company prides itself on teamwork and equality among its partners, a concept they reinforce with an egalitarian company structure that lincludes equal pay (and an expectation of equal contribution) for partners. The firm also touts its high partner-to-company ratio and commitment to the long-term in company development.

Benchmark Capital manages more than $2 billion in venture capital.

Investment Strategy

Benchmark Capital is interested in early-state technology companies that have exceptional potential for growth. In the technology sector, Benchmark invests in enterprise software and services, communications and security, semiconductors, mobile computing, consumer services and financial services. Using what it calls a "service-oriented" approach, the firm invests anywhere from $100,000 to $15 million in its companies. Its most common investment size is $3 million to $5 million as initial investment and a $5 million to $15 million investment during the life of the firm's engagement with the company.

Boston Millennia Partners

30 Rowes Wharf, Suite 500
Boston, MA 02110
www.millenniapartners.com

The Scoop

Millennia Partners was established in 1982. Since 1994, it has grown to four times its original size. Millennia provides companies with its industry knowledge, global network and organizational development services, as well as assistance with the search for leading management.

Millennia Partners has completed over 160 acquisitions, and set up 18 IPOs for its portfolio companies. The company does business in 15 countries, specializing in healthcare, life science, communication and IT and business services.

Investment Strategy

Millennia identifies "core companies." Necessary characteristics include having recognition in the market and some kind of advantage, technological or otherwise, within a rapidly transforming industry. A core company must also have the potential to earn at least $50 million annually within five years.

Millennia Partners' "core company strategy" involves consolidating companies around an existing business. Millennia prefers to be the leading investor in a company. Their primary investment is anywhere from $3 million to $10 million, and can be up to $15 million for one company. The firm invests in companies located in the United States as well as Canada, though they prefer to invest in companies located in the eastern U.S.

Canaan Partners

2884 Sand Hill Road, Suite 115
Menlo Park, CA 94025
www.canaan.com

The Scoop

Canaan Partners has been in business since 1987. The firm conducts bi-costal operations in California and Connecticut. The firm's team consists of professionals that have comprehensive experience in the sector in which they invest, and most of the associates have been working together for more than 10 years.

Canaan strives for full understanding of any company in which they plan to invest. There is a time period of four to six weeks in which the firm evaluates the management team backgrounds, product market strength and capital requirements for the goals set, as well as other components of a company.

Canaan manages $2 billion in capital and has invested in over 100 companies.

Investment Strategy

Canaan funds companies in the following sectors: communication, software and services, semiconductors and electronics, financial services, and life science. Chosen companies must demonstrate "innovative ideas, strong management teams and intriguing business models." Canaan focuses on creating long-term partnerships with companies. The firm invests in companies in all stages of development, but specializes in start-up and emerging-growth companies. Canaan's investment levels range from $4 million to $20 million.

ComVentures

305 Lytton Avenue
Palo Alto, CA 94308
www.comventures.com

The Scoop

Founded in 1974, ComVentures focuses on investment in the communication and infrastructure companies. The firm invests during the early-stage of a company's development, and focuses on identifying profitable innovation and breakthrough technology.

The firm has invested in over 175 early-stage companies and manages $1.5 billion in capital.

Investment Strategy

ComVentures is usually the first venture capital firm to invest in a company. The firm prides itself on being adept at helping a company anticipate and react strategically to change. From refining the vision of the company to developing strong financial strategies, ComVentures' goal is to elevate a company to a market leader.

Domain Associates

One Palmer Square, Suite 515
Princeton, NJ 08542
www.domainvc.com

The Scoop

Since its founding 19 years ago, Domain Associates has invested in 160 companies and now manages $1.4 billion in capital. The firm specializes in early-stage, life science companies. Domain looks for companies that have a technological benefit and can provide new solutions to the needs of the market, as well as an excellent executive team leading the company. The firm prefers to take part in the first round of financing, and takes an active role in their investment, usually assuming a seat on a company's board of directors.

Investment Strategy

Domain Associates invests in both private companies, and through their public equity fund, in small healthcare companies that may have been overlooked by other investors. Although they are small, these companies in Domain's portfolios are poised for a big advancement, either clinically or commercially. The firm also invests in creating companies from the ground up.

Draper Fisher Jurvetson

2882 Sand Hill Road
Menlo Park, CA 94025
www.dfj.com

The Scoop

Draper Fisher Jurvetson was established in 1985. The name Draper has a long history in the field. Timothy C. Draper, the firm's founder, is a third generation venture capitalist. His grandfather General William H. Draper Jr. created the Marshall plan as Undersecretary of the U.S. Army and founded the first venture capital firm on the West Coast in 1958. William H. Draper III, Tim Draper's father, also had his own VC firm.

DFJ concentrates on the technology of the companies it invests in, seeking innovators and companies that serve large, emerging markets. With affiliate companies and offices all over the world, the firm controls $3 billion in capital.

Investment Strategy

DFJ invests mainly in early-stage companies, usually serving as the first investor. DFJ's portfolio includes companies in such sectors as computing software to financial services to networking. The firm seeks companies that cater to fast-growing new markets, as well as those that produce new products to serve estalished markets in a new and better way. In DFJ's strategy, a great emphasis is placed on hiring the best people. DFJ also tries to build relationships with consumers of the companies they are sponsoring. This gives them feedback about the services that their investment is providing. The final goal of the DFJ is to take a company public.

Flagship Ventures

150 CambridgePark Drive, 10th Floor
Cambridge, MA 02140
www.flagshipventures.com

The Scoop

Flagship Ventures was founded in 1999. The firm is bi-coastal, with offices in Massachusetts and California. The 16 professionals that make up the Flagship team come together from different backgrounds: academic, technical, executive, and venture capital, to make investment decisions. The firm makes investments in four sectors: information technology, life science, nanotechnology, and communication. Flagship is responsible for funding 30 start-up companies and providing financing for over 100 more. The firm controls $800 million in capital.

Investment Strategy

Flagship Ventures typically serves as the lead investor when working with companies. The firm usually becomes involved at the seed or the first round of financing. The investment level generally ranges from $250,000 to $7 million. Though a typical investment is $2.5 million to $5 million, Flagship can invest up to $20 million in a company it is financing.

Foundation Capital

70 Willow Road, Suite 200
Menlo Park, CA 94025
www.foundationcapital.com

The Scoop

Founded in 1995, Foundation Capital invests in innovators in the following sectors: telecommunications and networking, Internet infrastructure, and enterprise software. The firm controls $1.1 billion in capital.

Investment Strategy

The firm places emphasis on helping new companies by introducing them to other potential investors, consumers and industry leaders. Foundation Capital begins to work with companies in their very early stage. The amount of the initial investment by Foundation Capital is anywhere from $1 million to $10 million. The firm generally continues its financing relationship by contributing to each of the following rounds of fundraising held by the company. Acting as leaders in financing rounds, members of Foundation Capital are often asked to take a seat on their companies' Boards of Directors.

GIMV

Karel Oomstraat 37
Antwerp, B-2018
www.gimv.com

The Scoop

GIMV was established in Belgium in 1980 and now has offices in The Hague, London and Frankfurt. GIMV focuses on three separate sectors for investment: corporate investments, life science, and information and communication technology. The firm's investment activity is spread throughout Europe as well as in the United States.

Investment Strategy

GIMV has three separate strategies for its three areas of interest.

In information and communication technology investments, GIMV seeks companies in early to mid stages of their development. The typical first investment is 2-5 million euros, and may reach 5-7 million euros for the life of the investment. In this sector GIMV invests in companies mainly in Benelux, France and the United Kingdom.

In the life science sector, GIMV concentrates on biotech companies. The companies are typically in their seed or early-stage phase of development and are in Europe or the U.S.

GIMV's corporate investments division focuses on mid-size companies for buy-outs and buy-ins. Initial investment by GIMV is no less than 2.5 million euros. The firm is expanding its horizons in this sector, investing in countries like Slovakia, Kazakhstan and Russia.

Intel Capital

2200 Mission College Blvd, RN6-37
Santa Clara, CA 95052
www.intel.com/capital

The Scoop

Created in the 1990s, Intel Capital is venture capital branch of Intel (the same Intel that made the Pentium processor in your computer). Though originally founded with the goal of helping its parent company by investing in companies that provided products for Intel's own production, the VC firm's goals soon expanded. ICap now invests in companies that advance technology for Internet users or bring new industries online.

Investment Strategy

Intel Capital has invested in over 1000 companies. Its main investment areas are the Internet and technology, with subcategories that include hardware and software, services and channels and component technology. ICap provides investment for companies in their early stages of development and guides them to their IPOs or acquisition by other companies. The firm may also continue working with a company on strategy even after it sells off its investments in the company.

ICap is usually a co-investor. Although the firm does most of its investing in the U.S., it seeks companies worldwide. Currently, 40 percent of ICap's investments are in businesses outside the U.S.

InterWest Partners

2710 Sand Hill Road, second floor
Menlo Park, CA 94025
www.interwest.com

The Scoop

InterWest Partners celebrated its 25th anniversary in 2004. From its first fund in 1979, which was $33.7 million, InterWest has grown significantly, currently investing out of InterWest VIII, with $750 million in funds.

The firm invests in two sectors: life science and technology. InterWest has financed more than 230 companies in these fields. Out of that total, 60 have made their initial public offerings and 30 have merged successfully with other companies.

InterWest now manages $1.6 billion in capital.

Investment Strategy

The firm prefers to invest in the early stages of a company, but will not pass up a good opportunity if a business is in its later stages. Once the company is in their portfolio, InterWest continues to invest through several rounds of financing. The firm is the lead investors in 70 percent of their ventures. InterWest will typically spend $10 million to $15 million during the life of an investment. Firm partners serve on the Board of Directors for 85 percent of the companies in InterWest's portfolio.

JPMorgan Partners

1221 Avenue of the Americas
New York, NY 10020
www.jpmorganpartners.com

The Scoop

JPMorgan Partners is a giant venture capital firm with a portfolio sprawling over five different sectors, offices all over the world, 95 investment professionals and $13 billion under management. Since JPMP formed in 1984, it has closed on more than 1,300 transactions. Even with such large volume, involvement in their companies is a high priority. JPMP partners serve as directors for 300 companies in the firm's portfolio.

Investment Strategy

The focus of JPMP is middle-market buy-outs, across the five sectors and across the world. JPMP's five segments of expertise are consumer, retail and service, financial services, industrial growth, life science and healthcare, and technology, media and telecom. Generally JPMP likes to lead with investments in management buy-outs within its sectors, providing $25 million- $200 million. JPMP invests in the medium to late stages of a company's growth, putting in $5 million to $150 million, except in the life science & healthcare sector, where the investments tend to be a bit smaller. JPMP also seeks financing opportunities in the early stages of life science companies, investing $3 million to $40 million.

Kleiner Perkins Caufield & Byers

2750 Sand Hill Road
Menlo Park, CA 94025
www.kpcb.com

The Scoop

Kleiner Perkins Caufield & Byers was established in 1972. Responsible for helping establish widely known companies such as Amazon, Compaq and Google, the firm has completed hundreds of transactions in financing, building up more than 350 companies. KPCB's partners have had real operations and management experience, which they tout as an advantage for nurturing an emerging company.

Kleiner Perkins Caufield & Byers recently closed its KPCB XI Fund with the amount of $400 million.

Investment Strategy

The firm's focus is early-stage companies in the technology sector. KPCB's portfolio includes many industries in the medical field, financial services, the Internet, and customer services and devices. Kleiner Perkins Caufield & Byers is careful not to invest in companies that compete with each other, so that the firm can give a company exclusive support and attention.

Kodiak Venture Partners

1000 Winter Street, Suite 3800
Waltham, MA 02451
www.kodiakvp.com

The Scoop

Kodiak Venture Partners was formed in 1999 in Massachusetts and specializes in investing in businesses on the East Coast of the U.S. With the goal of transforming start-up companies into industry leaders, the firm's partners apply many years of experience as entrepreneurs, investors and executives. Kodiak manages and trades from three funds that total $676 million.

Investment Strategy

Technology-focused, the firm invests in communication/IT, semiconductors and software. Kodiak begins to invest in the earliest stage of the company's formation. It helps with all the critical steps that lead to getting ahead of competitors: creating a business strategy, recruiting a winning executive team, and developing a network of customers and professionals in the field.

Mayfield

2800 Sand Hill Road, Suite 250
Menlo Park, CA 94025
www.mayfield.com

The Scoop

Mayfield Ventures was founded more than four decades ago. Since then it's been busy, financing companies out of 11 fundsand investing in 455 companies. Out of those, more 100 companies have completed their initial public offerings, and more than 150 were aided in mergers and acquisitions. With a specialization in technology, Mayfield takes credit for helping the development and growth of Silicone Valley through investment in key companies.

Mayfield has also set up funds to share some of their wealth with the community. One of the funds gives money to non-profit organizations such as museums and social services. Another fund is a fellowship program for engineering students who have entrepreneurship interests.

Mayfield controls over $2.1 billion in capital.

Investment Strategy

In the technology sector, Mayfield specializes in communication and customer and enterprise software. They begin their relationship with companies in the incubation, seed or early stages. Mayfield looks for innovative ideas, an understanding of market needs, as well as deep knowledge of technology. Mayfield also demands a proven business strategy to be followed by its companies.

Menlo Ventures

3000 Sand Hill Rd, Bldg. 4, Ste. 100
Menlo Park, CA 94025
www.menloventures.com

The Scoop

One of the oldest firms in Silicon Valley, Menlo Ventures has more than 28 years of experience in the venture capital industry. The firm has raised nine funds since its founding, and has invested in more than 300 companies. Menlo currently manages a total of $2.6 billion. Though their portfolio is varied, Menlo is currently placing emphasis on the technology sector.

Investment Strategy

Menlo invests in the following fields within the technology sector: communications, software, Internet infrastructure, semiconductor, data storage, and computer hardware companies. The firm invests in all stages of a company's life cycle. A typical investment for a startup company is $5 million to $10 million. For a later stage company the typical investment is $10 million to $25 million. Menlo funds U.S. companies exclusively. The firm keeps close ties with the companies they finance, serving on boards of 85 percent of their portfolio companies.

Mobius Venture Capital

200 West Evelyn Avenue, Suite 200
Mountain View, CA 94043
www.mobiusvc.com

The Scoop

Another successful West Coast firm, Mobius Venture Capital controls $1.25 billion in capital. The firm invests in the technology sector, 65 percent in California, 20 percent in the Midwest and the remaining 15 percent in East Coast cities.

The people of Mobius have experience from a range of backgrounds, as CEOs, entrepreneurs and top technology executives. Each investment decision is made by the team as a whole so all the different perspectives can be considered to yield the best possible outcome.

Investment Strategy

Mobius invests mainly in early-stage companies in 10 specializations within the technology sector. In two-thirds of its ventures, Mobius is the first investor. The firm seeks to own a large share (at least 20 percent) of the company after their investment. Mobius leads funding efforts with typical investments of $2 million to $5 million for early-stage companies and up to $15 million in later stages.

MPM Capital

111 Huntington Avenue
Boston, MA 02199
www.mpmcapital.com

The Scoop
MPM Capital is the largest investor in life science companies in the world. The firm has a total of $2.1 billion under management. MPM seeks out innovations in healthcare, investing equally in private and public equity. The firm invests out of two funds, delivering large returns from their ventures due to strategic integration of public and private funding.

Investment Strategy
Within its life science sector, MPM specializes in biotechnology / biopharmaceuticals and medical technology.

Currently, MPM is investing out of BioVentures III, a fund that controls $900 million and is one of the biggest funds dedicated to life science in the world. The firm is building a portfolio of 40 to 45 companies mainly in the biotechnology field. Approximately 20 percent of the investments from this fund will be made outside the U.S. In the past, investment sizes have varied, with anywhere between $7 million to $50 million invested per company.

New Enterprise Associates

2490 Sand Hill Road
Menlo Park, CA 94025
www.nea.com

The Scoop
New Enterprise Associates (NEA) formed in 1978. It has since invested in 500 companies; 145 of these have gone public and 185 have been acquired by other companies. NEA has accumulated $6 billion in capital under management, and operates with three offices around the United States.

Some of the ways in which NEA contributes to the growth of its companies: recruitment of leading management, introducing companies to vendors and consumers, identifying problems and solutions for the progress of the company, and setting up meetings between CEOs to share their experiences and learn from each other.

Investment Strategy
The firm specializes in technology and healthcare. NEA begins its investments in all stages of companies' development, but prefers invest in early-stage companies. The firm is the leader in 90% of its investments, raising the capital for the companies and finding them new investors. NEA typically continues financing its portfolio companies in subsequent financing rounds. In fact, the typical relationship between NEA and a company is five to seven years. The range of investment is $200,000 to $40 million.

Northwest Venture Associates

221 North Wall Street, Suite 628
Spokane, WA 99201
www.nwva.com

The Scoop

The U.S. Northwest is a growing region for industry, partly due to local universities' research launching innovative businesses. For the past 15 years, Northwest Venture Associates (NWVA) has been cultivating these start-ups in Washington, Oregon, Idaho and Montana. The firm invests out of three funds, the last of which was formed in 2000, with total funds of $133 million.

Investment Strategy

NWVA invests in three sectors: software, communications and consumer business. In the past two years, the firm has been most actively investing in the state of Washington. Typical investments range from $500,000 to $10 million. NWVA invests in companies at all stages, but prefers the first round of financing because it allows them to participate in the launch of new products and monitor the formation of relationships between company and consumer. NWVA also has several other venture firms with which they partner when investing in companies. These relationships spread the cost of the investment between several firms and lessen investment risk, also benefitting the company by providing more than one partnership and strategic option.

Norwest Venture Partners

525 University Avenue, Suite 800
Palo Alto, CA 94301-1922
www.nvp.com

The Scoop

Norwest Venture Partners (NVP) has been in business for more than 40 years. In that time, it has developed a specialization in information technology. Having invested in 350 companies, the firm has gathered and manages $1.8 billion in venture capital.

The funds of NVP range in size and the year they were established. The oldest fund was formed in 1985, and the largest and most recent is a 2001 fund totalling $411 million.

Investment Strategy

NVP is usually the lead investor in its portfolio companies. The firm begins its investment in the seed or early stage of a company. The firm goes on to invest totals of $10 million to $15 million per company through many stages of investment, but there is the possibility of investment anywhere from $3 million to $25 million. NVP's 2003 investments provide a good example of the firm's investment strategy: out of the $59 million NVP invested, $11 million went to companies that were making a first-time appearance in NVP's portfolio, and the remaining $48 million went to follow-up investment for companies already in its portfolio.

Oak Investment Partners

One Gorham Island
Westport, CT 06880
www.oakinv.com

The Scoop

Oak Investment Partners have 25 years of experience in the venture capital business. Still, the firm is not above investment advice from industry professionals. Oak Investment Partners maintains a network of 250 experts in different fields at the ready.

The firm has achieved a strong track record for successful investment: having interacted with 350 companies through investment, the firm currently holds $5.8 billion in committed capital.

Investment Strategy

Oak Investment Partners has diversified its investments into several different sectors, including technology and software, healthcare and retail. The firm typically invests in the mid to late stages of a company's development, as well as in buy-outs. Oak Investment Partners will usually invest $30 million to $60 million in later stages of a company or in special circumstances, and $10 million to $25 million in the early stages. Oak looks for an excellent management team in companies it finances. Also, Oak Investment Partners mainly does business with people or entities with which they have woked before, or to whom they have been referred by a trusted source.

Partech International

50 California Street, Suite 3200
San Francisco, CA 94111
www.partechvc.com

The Scoop

With 22 years of experience, Partech International has developed into a global venture capital firm. Partech has offices in San Francisco and Paris, France; its international offices provides an international perspective on choosing the most promising companies.

Partech manages approximately $850 million.

Investment Strategy

Partech specializes, and has deep expertise in enterprise software and communications, two of the fastest growing sectors of technology in the global economy. The firm invests in all stages of a company's development and typically continues its support through several financing rounds.

Polaris Venture Partners

1000 Winter Street, Suite 3350
Waltham, MA 02451-1215
www.polarisventures.com

The Scoop

Polaris Ventures was founded in 1996. The firm currently holds 70 companies in their portfolio, and has over $2 billion under management. Through Polaris headquarters' close proximity to MIT, they have formed a strong relationship with the famed MIT Media Lab. Polaris has funded more companies started in the MIT Media Lab than any other VC firm.

Investment Strategy

Polaris helps establish leaders in the life science and information technology sector. The technology focus occupies a majority of their investments, comprising 53 percent of their portfolio. Investments in life science make up another 32 percent, and the rest, 13 percent, is invested in the growth equity sector. Polaris usually provides the seed money or begins investment in the early stages of the company. Since Polaris is the leader or co-leader in mostly all their investments, it participates extensively in growing their portfolio companies.

Prism Venture Partners

100 Lowder Brook Drive Suite 2500
Westwood MA 02090
www.prismventure.com

The Scoop

Prism Venture Capital was founded in 1996. Since that time, the firm has raised four funds yielding $1 billion in funds and has invested in more than 50 start-ups. Prism doesn't just look for profitable ventures externally; it also continue to launch their own companies in-house. Since the firm's founding, Prism partners have created three companies that are typical of the Prism emphasis on market-transforming technology and seizing underserved markets. Prism also encourages communication between the companies in its portfolio, organizing meetings between upper management at least once a year to network and discuss industry innovations.

Investment Strategy

Prism Ventures invests primarily in U.S. companies, and specializes in communications, business infra-structure software and systems, and life science technology. Prism likes to begin its investment in the early stage of the company, but if the right company presents itself, Prism invests in late-stage opportunities as well. A primary investment in a company is usually between $5 million and $10 million. An ideal company should have the potential to rise to an annual revenue of $100 million within five years. The company should also deliver services to a market that is growing quickly or whose needs have not yet been met.

Redpoint Ventures

3000 Sand Hill Road, Building 2
Suite 290
Menlo Park, CA 94025
www.redpoint.com

The Scoop

Operating since 1999, Redpoint Venture was founded by two general partners from Brentwood Venture Capital and Institutional Venture Partners, respectively. The founders describe the firm's three guiding principles: a passion for innovation, a commitment to partnership and shared vision, and an ability to network with an array of experts.

Investment Strategy

Redpoint Ventures concentrates on the technology sectors of communication infrastructure and software. Redpoint looks for companies that can become a platform company for the industry. The firm invests at the seed or early stage of a company and occasionally at the second stage. Redpoint's investment amounts range from $100,000 for seed money to $20 million for developed companies. Redpoint is the leader or co-leader in a large majority of its investments.

Rho Capital Partners

Carnegie Hall Tower
152 West 57th Street, 23rd Floor
New York, NY 10019
www.rho.com

The Scoop

Rho Ventures was founded in 1981. The firm has invested in more than 170 companies and today manages funds that collectively exceed $1 billion. The firm is currently investing out of Rho Ventures IV, launched in 2000, with an amount of $435 million raosed. Rho has invested in a number of well-known companies including Compaq, Commerce One, iVillage and Human Genome Sciences.

Investment Strategy

Rho Ventures invests in communications /hardware, information technology, healthcare and disruptive technologies. The firm invests in all stages of the company's development, from seed to IPO. The firm seeks companies that demonstrate great differentiation from the rest of the sector. Rho also looks for the potential of surpassing $500 million in annual revenue, a well-defined business model, and an exceptional management team.

Sequoia Capital

3000 Sand Hill Road, Bldg. 4
Suite 280
Menlo Park, CA 94025
www.sequoiacap.com

The Scoop
Sequoia Capital operates out of two offices, one in Menlo Park California, and the other, recently opened, in Israel. Sequoia was founded in 1972. Famous companies that have been funded by Sequoia include Electronic Arts and Yahoo!

The firm has distilled the art of investing down to a few tips it offers companies seeking financing. First, the firm asks whether an entrepreneur can write her business plan on the back of a business card. Second, a company should have a good sense of who exactly will be consuming their product. Finally, is theirs a good or service the consumer can't live without?

Investment Strategy
Sequoia Capital invests in the tech categories of components, systems, and software and services. The firm makes 8 to 12 new investments a year and 12 to 15 follow-up investments a year. The financing is usually offered to early-stage companies that are West of the Rockies, more mature companies in the areas around Boston and Dallas, and early-stage companies in Israel.

Sequoia seeks companies that address a large market and meet an undeniable consumer need. The firm emphasizes the values of thriftiness and unconventionality, noting they are often typical of successful companies.

Sevin Rosen Funds

Two Galleria Tower
13455 Noel Road, Suite 75240
Dallas, TX 75240
www.srfunds.com

The Scoop
Sevin Rosen Funds has been in business since 1981. The firm operates out of four offices, two in Texas and two in California. SRF is dedicated to bringing technological advances to the market by funding companies and entrepreneurs. The firm shows its dedication not only through venture capital, but also through scholarships. Together with University of California-Berkeley, Sevin Rosen Funds awards a scholarship to engineering students who demonstrate technical innovation.

SRF recently closed its Sevin Rosen Fund IX, raising $305 million to be invested in technology companies. This latest fund brings the firm's total amount under management to $1.8 billion.

Investment Strategy
Within the technology sector, SFI invests in the following categories: semiconductor /computing, software and services, and telecommunications. The firm invests in the very early stages of its companies, funding the incubation or the seed phases.

Sierra Ventures

2884 Sand Hill Road, Suite 100
Menlo Park, CA 94025
www.sierraventures.com

The Scoop

Like so many other leading venture capital firms, Sierra Ventures calls Menlo Park, California, home. Sierra began operations in 1982, concentrating on information technology companies. The firm has $1.1 billion of committed capital, which it holds through eight partnerships. The earliest of these partnerships was started back in 1985, and the latest closed in 2000. Sierra ventures makes decisions as a team; all managing partners must reach consensus when choosing an investment. There is also a support network of lawyers, finance professionals and industry experts providing support for the firm and their portfolio companies.

Investment Strategy

Within the information technology sector, Sierra Ventures focuses on enterprise software, Internet infrastructure, semiconductors and telecommunications hardware, and software and services. The firm invests during the early to mid-stages of the company's development, with funding totalling $10 million to $15 million for a single company, paid during several rounds of funding. The firm looks for companies that make a minimum of $1 million in quarterly revenue.

Sofinnova Partners

17, rue de Surene
Paris, 75008
www.sofinnova.fr

The Scoop

Sofinnova Partners began in 1972 as a Paris-based venture capital firm. In 1997, they opened a sister firm called Sofinnova Ventures in San Francisco. The two entities operate separately, but do combine investment efforts where appropriate. Sofinnova Partners manages assets worth 500 million euros, held in four funds. The latest fund is their biggest and holds 330 million euros. The firm invests mostly in Europe. Sofinnova Partners plans to spend roughly 40 percent of its latest fund in Paris, 35 percent to 40 percent in the rest of Europe and approximately 15 percent in the United States.

Investment Strategy

Sofinnova Partners invests exclusively in various divisions of the life science and information technology sectors. The firm starts their relationship with the company in the early stages of development and continues their funding in subsequent stages, with a toal investment amount of between 12 million to 15 million euros.

The firm receives about 1,500 business plans a year, and only closely examines about 20 percent of these. The companies that get the attention of Sofinnova Partners are producing break-through products capable of changing the market, and are managed by able executive teams.

Sofinnova Ventures

140 Geary Street, 10th Floor
San Francisco, CA 94108
www.sofinnova.com

The Scoop

Sofinnova Ventures, though based in San Francisco, has deep roots in the European market. Sofinnova was started in 1997 by its French namesake and the oldest venture capital firm in France. Due to this special relationship, Sofinnova Ventures has a unique transatlantic advantage and is well positioned to help American companies enter the European market. Likewise, Sofinnova opens doors for European companies entering the American market.

The firm, which was started in 1997 with $57 million under management now controls $600 million.

Investment Strategy

Sofinnova Ventures invests in the information technology and life science sectors. About 66 percent of the firm's investment funds go toward information technology companies and 34 percent toward ventures in life science. A large majority of companies the firm finances are in their early stage of development, 8 percent are in their seed period and 8 percent are in later stages. Out of the companies that Sofinnova Ventures funds, 90 percent are in the United States in the San Francisco, San Diego and Seattle areas. The rest of the companies are located in Europe.

Sofinnova Ventures is often a leader or a co-leader in an investment, though the firm prefers to share an investment with other strong venture firms.

Split Rock Partners

10400 Viking Drive
Suite 550
Minneapolis, MN 55344
www.splitrockpartners.com

The Scoop

In June of 2004, St. Paul Ventures split into two independent venture capital firms, Split Rock Partners and Vesbridge Partners.

Split Rock Partners now invests in healthcare, software and internet companies. SplitRock's headquarters are in Minneapolis, with an additional office in Menlo Park.

Investment Strategy

Split Rock Partners seeks out early-stage companies and usually leads or co-leads financing. The firm's investment reach covers the upper Midwest and the West Coast. Split Rock becomes greatly involved with companies they finance, serving on their boards and providing an extensive support network of resources.

Sprout Group

11 Madison Avenue, 13th Floor
New York, NY 10010
www.sproutgroup.com

The Scoop

Established in 1969, Sprout Group has had a long, fulfilling history, helping to establish such well-known companies as mySimon, Staples and VeriFone, among others. The firm has made investments in more than 350 companies, whose combined revenue today is more than $50 billion. In November of 2000 Sprout closed its biggest fund yet: Sprout IX, containing $1.1 billion.

The firm has raised $3 billion in committed capital .

Investment Strategy

Sprout Group invests in the following sectors: communication, software and healthcare technology, in all stages of their development. Sprout is typically a leader or a co-leader in their investments; the firm has led in 73 percent of its investments in the last five years. Sprout invests with other firms who have similar visions for a company. The firm takes a participatory approach in the companies they finance, occupying seats on the board of directors in 79 percent of their companies, also participating in key decisions, developing strategies and hiring management.

Sutter Hill Ventures

755 Page Mill Road, A-200
Palo Alto, CA 94304
www.shv.com

The Scoop

Sutter Hill Ventures has been passionate about building companies since 1962. Not just looking for a quick "flip," Sutter Hill stresses their commitment to putting in the time necessary to successfully launch a company. Sutter Hill assists with market research and provides CEOs and management full access to the advice and opinions of the Sutter Hill team.

The firm holds $500 million under management.

Investment Strategy

Sutter Hill invests in companies located all over the United States occupying a number of sectors: consumer, software, healthcare, business and financial services. The firm mostly funds companies in the latter fields that are technology-based. The firm takes great interest in early-stage companies and touts their hands-on approach to developing companies. In addition to financial support, they also give assistance with assembling a winning management team, distributing funds, and developing a business model.

Techno Venture Management

Maximilianstr. 35, Entrance C
Munich, D-80539
Germany
www.tvmvc.com

The Scoop

Techno Venture Management, founded in 1983, was one of the first venture capital firms to operate in Germany. The firm opened a U.S. office in Boston in 1986. Techno Venture specializes in transatlantic investments, creating companies that are active on both sides of the ocean. The firm has invested in more than 220 companies in Europe and the United States, many of which have gone public.

The firm manages a total of 918 million euros.

Investment Strategy

Although Techno Venture Management invests in the IT & communication sectors, as well as in life science, the most recently raised fund concentrates on telecommunication and information technology. Techno Venture is currently investing out of its seventh fund, TVM V information technology, formed in 2002 and worth 128 million euros. The firm invests in companies in all stages of their development, from seed to mature stages.

TL Ventures

435 Devon Park Drive, 700 Building
Wayne, PA 19087-1945
www.tlventures.com

The Scoop

Fifteen years after its inception, TL Ventures has come a long way. The firm has invested in over 185 companies, out of which 45 companies have completed their IPOs, and 70 companies are still active in their portfolio. The firm holds over $1.4 billion under management.

The investing team prides itself on the extensive assistance it offers companies. Available for guidance themselves, the firm also has a large network of experts available for consultation. The TL team is personally familiar with the challenges faced by entrepreneurs; most of the firm's partners created their own businesses and led them either to IPOs or to a successful merger or acquisition.

Investment Strategy

TL Ventures has offices in Texas, Pennsylvania and California and targets investments in those regions. The firm concentrates in technology in the fields of communication, biotechnology, information technology and software. TL looks for companies in their early stages of development and cultivates the company through assistance with market and product development.

Trident Capital

505 Hamilton Avenue, Suite 200
Palo Alto, CA 94301
www.tridentcapital.com

The Scoop

Trident Capital has been in operation since 1993. The firm has organized five funds and manage $1.2 billion of capital. Trident Capital attributes its success to their ability to analyze the market and choose the leaders of tomorrow,.with investment in companies like MapQuest and CSG Systems.

Investment Strategy

The focus of Trident Capital is information and business services, with current emphasis on companies that provide marketing services, work on infrastructure within the wireless and information security networks, and IT companies outsourcing their business. Trident invests in all stages of the company, preferring to choose investments based on the overall quality of an enterprise rather than on a stage of development.

US Venture Partners

2735 Sand Hill Road
Menlo Park, CA 94025
www.usvp.com

The Scoop

US Venture Partners (USVP) has done well for itself since its founding in 1981. The firm's specializations in the Internet and technology have led to investments in more than 370 companies, 69 of which have completed IPOs. USVP prides themselves on being the founding investors in such successful companies as Sun Microsystems and Stratacom/Cisco, among many others. The firm's 16 members have more than 200 years of management experience and includes seven former CEOs and two PhDs.

Investment Strategy

USVP invests in early-stage companies in the Internet, communications, software, semiconductors, medical and consumer branded sectors. The typical seed money investment for a company is $500, 000. In the later stages of a company's development an investment can reach as high as $10 million, but the typical range of an investment is from $4 million to $5 million.

USVP is very hands-on and continually reevaluates its investments. The partners of the firm regularly attend the board meetings of the companies in which they invest, usually more than one partner at a time. The companies are reviewed every quarter by USVP and their progress is tracked and recorded. From this, the firm decides if more funding is needed, as well as what other aid can be given to drive their investment to success.

VantagePoint Venture Partners

1001 Bayhill Drive, Suite 300
San Bruno, CA 94066
www.vpvp.com

The Scoop

VantagePoint Venture Partners specializes in tech companies. The sole or co-leading investor for more than 100 companies, VantagePoint is also one of the most active and largest venture capital firms in the world and has helped 400 companies go public. The firm holds $2.8 billion under management.

The investment professionals of VantagePoint have more than 300 years of experience between them. The firm has developed a 'Partner-Team' approach to helping its portfolio companies – the firm offers a broad range of services to its companies, including marketing, finance help and executive training.

Investment Strategy

VantagePoint is a multi-stage investor, investing in the early stages, later stages, and right up to the completion of an IPO. The firm seeks investments that will require anywhere from $25 million to $150 million to complete their IPO. VantagePoint likes to be the sole provider of funding necessary for a company.

Venrock Associates

30 Rockefeller Plaza
Room 5508
New York, NY 10112
www.venrock.com

The Scoop

Venrock Associates was officially established in 1969, though its roots go back more than 30 years to venture capital activities started by the Rockefeller family. Since its inception, the firm has invested $1.3 billion in more than 340 companies. Venrock takes pride in building household names such as Apple Computers, 3M and Intel, among many others.

Investment Strategy

Venrock Associates concentrates in healthcare and technology, seeking cutting edge ideas capable of being transformed into great returns for investors. Venrock starts its relationship with companies early on and maintains support until the later stages. Venrock involve its whole firm in each investment by presenting each company to all firm partners during the investment process.

Venrock has offices on both coasts and invests in companies regardless of locale.

Versant Ventures

3000 Sand Hill Road, Suite 260
Menlo Park, CA 94025
www.versantventures.com

The Scoop

Versant Ventures is a West Coast firm dedicated to financing early-stage companies that address different needs of the medical and life science sectors. Versant currently holds $650 million in committed capital: $250 million through its first fund, Versant Ventures I, and the remaining $400 million from Versant Ventures II.

Investment Strategy

Versant has very selective criteria when choosing companies worthy of investment. Whether the company is putting new, cutting-edge technology on the market or has discovered how to do something better, faster and cheaper, the same principles apply. Versant chooses their investments by examining the management team of the company, their vision, the solidity of their business plan, and the competitiveness of whatever the company produces in the marketplace. The firm also evaluates the potential for growth and the readiness of leaders to build a large company. Versant looks for companies that have the potential of making between $100 million and $500 million in annual revenue within a few years.

Vestbridge Partners

1700 West Park Drive
Westboro, MA 01581
www.vestrbridge.com

The Scoop

In June of 2004, St. Paul Ventures split into two independent venture capital firms, Split Rock Partners and Vesbridge Partners.

Vesbridge Partners focuses on networking technologies and information technology and is headquartered in Boston.

Investment Strategy

Vesbridge Partners invests in early-stage companies in the IT field. The firm looks for a strong management team, a large market that is addressed by the products or services offered by the company, and a unique business model. The firm invests typically from $5 million to $30 million over several stages of investment.

CAREERS

APPENDIX

VENTURE CAPITAL

Venture Capital Networking Groups

Business School VC Conferences

- Columbia, Harvard and Wharton all hold annual Private Equity Conferences

National VC Conferences (Hosts)

- Golden Capital Network (GCN)—Western states (www.goldencapital.net)
- Strategic Research Institute—National (www.srinstitute.com)
- Institute for International Research (IIR)—National (www.iirusa.com/Finance)
- International Business Forum (IBF)—National (www.ibfconferences.com)

Angel Groups (Because most angel groups are very loosely-structured organizations, the majority will not have sufficient infrastructure in place to hire any employees. They should however play an invaluable networking role in your quest to meeting venture capitalists who do [hire].)

- National:
  - ACE-Net (www.ace-net.org)
  - Tribe of Angels: (www.tribeofangels.com)
- West:
  - Band of Angels (www.bandangels.com)
  - Sacramento Angels (www.sacangels.com)
  - Sierra Angels (www.sierraangels.com)
- Midwest:
  - Saint Louis Angels
  - (http://www.technologygateway.org/resources.asp)
- East:
  - Walnut Venture Associates: (www.walnutventures.com)

Regional Technology Alliances (mostly West Coast public/private partnerships bringing together venture capitalists, entrepreneurs, and service providers in a networking and support environment)

- Sacramento and Northern California (www.sarta.org)
- Los Angeles (www.larta.org)
- San Diego (www.sdrta.org)

Glossary

Carry: A percentage of the profits the firm makes. Carry is the Holy Grail of venture capital. Typically, the general partners receive a combined 20 percent of the profit from investing. For instance, if a firm receives $100 million in capital for its fund, and over 10 years returns $400 million, the profit was $300 million. The investors, or limited partners, receive 80 percent or $240 million, and the general partners split 20 percent or $60 million among themselves. Some premier VC firms have reportedly raised carry to 30 percent.

Closing: After the due diligence is done, and the VC finally decides to invest in the company, there is a legal closing of the deal. Involving lawyers and large contracts, the process can take one to four weeks.

Closing bonus: A bonus often given to lower-level employees for sourcing or doing due diligence on deals that are done. This is intended to focus their attention on the best deals and work hard to get them closed.

Co-investment: A common program through which employees can invest their own money alongside the firm in some or all of the portfolio companies. If a firm is successful, the upside to this program can far exceed the salary and bonuses.

Cramdown: An unfortunately common occurrence when times are bad, where current-round investors seriously dilute all former shareholders by decreasing current share price to a small fraction of its former self.

Crater: A company that received venture capital and subsequently went bankrupt.

Crossover Fund: Most often a private equity fund with a core competency other than early stage VC, that has "crossed over" to include early stage startups on their radar.

Dog (also affectionately known as the "walking dead"): A company that received venture capital but is failing or going nowhere. "You can combine a dog with another dog, but you're still going to have a dog."

Due diligence: The process of investigating a company before investing in it. It typically includes calling references, calling customers, investigating competitors, validating legal contracts, visiting remote locations, coordinating with other investors, interviewing the entire management team, testing the technology, building spreadsheets and running sensitivity analyses on the projections to see if they make sense, etc.

Entrepreneur-in-residence: see Venture partner.

Exit: This is a liquidity event, or series of events, that allows a VC firm to turn the equity it owns in a company back into cash. That event is usually a sale of the company to a larger corporation, or an IPO that permits the firm to sell its shares. Typically, the VC cannot exit at the time of an IPO because they are "locked up" by the investment banks executing the IPO [see "lock up"].

Fund: The pool of money a venture capital firm raises to invest. Limited partners typically commit this money for a period of 10 years. Not to worry – the money does not sit in a bank account for ten years. In practice, the money is "drawn down" by the general partners as they need it (think "just-in-time"). Thus, most of the money stays with the limited partners, earning whatever rate of return they can achieve, until it is transferred to the VC for investment within a few weeks.

General partner: A partner in a VC firm. This is the person making the investment decisions and sitting on the boards of portfolio companies.

IPO: Initial Public Offering. Also known as "going public." When a company first issues equity shares for purchase by the public on one of the public exchanges.

IRR: Internal Rate of Return. A calculation that determines the rate of return on a portfolio investment or the total venture fund. If, for example, you put your money in a bank account that gives you 5.5 percent interest annually, you could say your IRR on that investment would be roughly 5.5 percent (not accounting for taxes or service fees). IRR is the most important measure of performance for a VC fund.

Limited partner: An investor in a VC fund. Typically, pension funds, endowments, wealthy individuals, and strategic investors such as large corporations that want access to the young companies in the VC's portfolio.

Limited partnership: The legal structure of many venture capital firms. It protects the investors in the fund from legal responsibility for things the fund managers might do. It also protects the partners by interference by investors for the duration of the fund, typically 10 years.

Lock-up: In an IPO, the venture capital firm is "locked-up" for a period of three to 18 months by the investment banks executing the public offering (typically 180 days). The VC firm is not allowed to sell shares on the public market during that time.

The reason for the lock-up? The market might see the VC selling shares as a negative signal. The job of the investment bank is to manage an orderly process that won't spook the market and have an adverse effect on the share price. Banks therefore get VCs to agree to a reasonable lock-up period.

Management fee: The general partners take a percentage of the fund every year to pay for expenses. Firms will on average charge the fund 1.5 to 2.5 percent. This pays for salaries, office space, travel, computers, phones, advertising, and legal expenses.

Partnership: Short for limited partnership.

Pre-money valuation: Value of the company before a VC invests capital. If, for example, a VC invests $2 million in a company and subsequently owns 25 percent of the company, then the pre-money value must have been $6 million. (2/X = .25. X thus equals 8, and since we know the VC firm added $2 million of value, the company must have been worth $8 – $2 = $6 million "pre-money.")

Post-money valuation: The value of the company after a VC invests capital. Example: if a VC invests $2 million in a company and subsequently owns 25 percent, the post-money valuation must have been $8 million. The VC added $2 million of value (now cash in the company's bank account) so $2/X=.25. X= $8 million.

SBIC: Small Business Investment Corporation. The U.S. Federal Government program that provides matching funds to venture capital firms to augment the amount they have available to invest. The SBIC program was created by the Small Business Investment Act of 1958. The Small Business Administration ("SBA") is the administrator for the program and is responsible for licensing SBICs. The program recognizes the efficacy of having private individuals, not the government, investing money in entrepreneurial ventures. Traditionally, venture funds that receive SBIC money have been considered lower-tier investors.

Soft-circled: Term used to describe potential limited partners and their money, when cash has been tentatively pledged to a new fund (but not yet invested or officially committed).

Sourcing: The process of finding investment opportunities. The person in a venture firm who does this well is very valuable to a firm. Because a deal may sometimes come from multiple sources simultaneously, there is often politicking within a VC firm to be credited with bringing a deal in the door. This is especially true when there is a bonus given for sourcing a deal that receives funding.

Term sheet (see attached sample): A high level (generally non-binding) funding offer prepared by a venture capital company summarizing the conditions and terms (of investment) the investor is prepared to accept. The term sheet covers the fundamental provisions of an investment and is often negotiated. Typical items in a term sheet include share price, percentage of ownership, monetary investment and changes to a company's charter and by laws.

Venture partner: An aspiring entrepreneur invited by a VC to hang out in their offices, use the phone, and use their networks to flesh out a business plan and build a management team. The VC will then provide initial funding to the venture. It's a way for a VC to build proprietary deal flow, and insure they are investing in the best entrepreneurs. It also helps the entrepreneurs by giving them a safe and credible place from which to investigate their ideas.

Sample Term Sheet

STARTUP, INC.
MEMORANDUM OF TERMS FOR PRIVATE PLACEMENT OF SERIES C PREFERRED STOCK
October, 2005

STARTUP, INC., a Delaware corporation (the **"Company"**) intends to sell and issue shares of its Series C Preferred Stock to Strategic Investor #1, VC Investors #1 through #4, and Angel Investors #1 through #3 (the **"Investors"**). This memorandum summarizes the principal terms proposed by the Company with respect to the private placement of Series C Preferred Stock to the Investors.

ISSUER:	STARTUP, INC. (THE "COMPANY"), A DELAWARE CORPORATION.	COMMENTS
Current Capitalization:		
Common Stock (as of 10/25/05)	11,772,342 shares	
Options on Common (as of 10/25/05)	11,634,933 shares	
Series A Preferred (as of 10/25/05)	3,240,907 shares (Common equivalent)	
Series B Preferred (as of 10/25/05)	12,098,254 shares (Common equivalent)	
Total shares outstanding	38,746,436 shares (Common and equivalent)	
Current Financing—Securities and Purchase Price:	Company is offering up to 21,105,621 shares of Series C Convertible Preferred Stock (the "Series C") at $1.28 per share, with an aggregate maximum offering of $27,000,000 at a pre-money valuation of $49,750,424. 38,746,436 shares (Common and equivalent)	
Purchasers:	Strategic Investor #1, VC Investors #1, #2, #3 and #4, Angel Investors #1, #2, and #3, collectively referred to as the "Investors."	

ISSUER:	STARTUP, INC. (THE "COMPANY"), A DELAWARE CORPORATION.	COMMENTS
Purchasers: Minimum Closing Amount:	$20,000,000	Gives investors an "out" or point of renegotiation if minimum is not reached.
Use of Proceeds:	The proceeds from the Investors' purchase of the Series C shall be used for capital expenditures and general purposes subject to the approval of the Board of Directors and Investors as prescribed herein.	
Initial Closing Date:	December 20, 2005, for not less than the minimum closing amount (with subsequent closing(s) thereafter, concluding no later than February 22, 2006).	Any period longer than 60-90 days (from initial closing) is excessive, since those who are late to the party would get the same terms with less risk (startups can come a long way in 90 days).
Dividends:	The holders of Series C Preferred Stock shall be entitled to receive an annual non-cumulative dividend, in preference to the Common Stock ("Common"), Series A and Series B, an approximate 8% (.08) return upon investment, respectively, when and if declared by the Board. After Series C has received all dividends duly required, the Series A and Series B shareholders shall then be entitled to receive an approximate 8% (.08) return upon investment, in dividends. Thereafter the common shareholders as a group are entitled to total gross dividends equal to the gross dividends issued to the Series A, B, and C Preferred shares multiplied by the total number of common shares	"Last cash in is the first cash out." Since current investors (Series C) take the greatest risk, they have negotiated for preferential treatment to other Preferred as well as Common.Common shareholders receive a weighted average dividend, with any additional funds split between all Common and Preferred. This is called "double dipping" by the Preferred shareholders.

ISSUER:	STARTUP, INC. (THE "COMPANY"), A DELAWARE CORPORATION.	COMMENTS
Dividends, cont.	outstanding and divided by the total number of Preferred shares on an as converted basis. Thereafter, the Series A, Series B and Series C Preferred shares (taken on an as converted basis) participate with Common shares as to dividends on a pro rata basis. Regardless, Common will receive no more than the Preferred, in the aggregate.	
Liquidation Preference:	In the event of any liquidation of the Company:First: Holders of the Series C Preferred shares shall be entitled to receive, in preference to the holders of Common, the Series A and Series B, an amount equal to 2.5x the original per share purchase price of their shares, plus any declared and unpaid dividends (unless converted into Common).Second: Holders of Series A and Series B Preferred shares shall be entitled to receive, in preference to the holders of Common, an amount equal to 2.5x the original purchase price of their shares then outstanding, together with any declared and unpaid dividends (unless converted into Common). Last: Any remaining proceeds shall be allocated between the holders of the common stock, the Series A and the Series B on a pro rata basis. A "Liquidation" shall be defined as any (a) sale, merger or other transaction which results in a Change of Control or (b) any liquidation or winding up of the Company.	Current investors get preferential treatment here as well, this time with respect to liquidity events (not including IPOs).In this deal, a multiple of 2.5x purchase price was negotiated.Once again, in order to mitigate risk (by increasing upside potential), Preferred Shareholders have negotiated a "double dipping" clause. This allows them to come back for seconds once Common Shareholders are next in line to be paid

ISSUER:	STARTUP, INC. (THE "COMPANY"), A DELAWARE CORPORATION.	COMMENTS
Mandatory Conversion:	The Series C will be subject to a mandatory conversion in the event of a Qualified IPO. A Qualified IPO is defined as one in which over $50 million in net proceeds is raised for the Company and the offering price per share is at least 300% of the Purchase Price per share of the Series C.	Although aggregate proceed minimums are necessary as a practical matter, they are a function of market forces and current economic climate.By setting a 300% of purchase price minimum, Series C investors are better able to protect their investment. Otherwise, prior investors who can get a nice return at today's share price might be more than happy with a Qualified IPO at or below the price/share paid by Series C.
Optional Conversion:	Series C Shareholders may convert, in whole or in part, at any time.	
Mandatory Redemption:	If no Liquidity Event has occurred by the fifth anniversary of the closing, the holders of the Series C will have the option for three years to redeem their holdings for an amount equal to the Aggregate Purchase Price (subject to appropriate adjustment in the event of any stock dividends, stock splits, combinations or other similar recapitalizations affecting such shares) plus the non-cumulative Dividend (including any accrued but unpaid dividends) and this amount (the "Redemption Amount") shall be paid in two equal installments at the dates of the one year and two year anniversaries of the date the holders exercise the option to redeem.	Forces Startup to buy back shares if no exit (IPO or M&A) has been reached within 5 years of this funding. This clause protects financial investors, but makes very many strategic investors extremely uneasy.

ISSUER:	STARTUP, INC. (THE "COMPANY"), A DELAWARE CORPORATION.	COMMENTS
Change of Control or Sale:	In the event of a (i) Change of Control (as defined below) or (ii) sale of a substantial portion of the Company's business or its assets, holders of the Series C shall have the option of (a) requiring the Company to redeem the Series C through payment of the Redemption Amount at the time of such an event or (b) converting the Series C. Change of Control shall mean a single transaction of series of transactions involving either (a) sale of equity securities or (b) merger or other combination of the Company which, in either case, results in shareholders (including the Investors) prior to such transaction or series of transactions owning less than 50% (assuming conversion of the Series C) of the voting equity securities of the Company or its successor after such a transaction or series of transactions.	Basic definition of Change in Control.
Anti-Dilution:	In the event the Company issues or is deemed to have issued additional shares of Common Stock, at a price per share less than the Series C Conversion Price, then the Series C Share Price shall be reduced by a full ratchet anti-dilution adjustment to such lesser price. There will be proportional adjustments for stock dividends, stock splits or other changes in capital structure.	Anti-dilution comes in two colors: Full ratchet and weighted average.The former means a full decrease in Series C price to match the new price, while the latter is self-explanatory.

ISSUER:	STARTUP, INC. (THE "COMPANY"), A DELAWARE CORPORATION.	COMMENTS
Voting Rights:	The holders of the Series C will have voting rights on an as-converted basis except as noted below under Approval Rights.	Basic definition of Change in Control.
Approval Rights:	In addition to voting rights on an as-converted basis, the following actions will require approval of the holders of at least 50% of the Series C: a. The creation of any preferred stock or convertible debt with rights or privileges senior to or pari passu with the Series C. b. The creation of any preferred stock or convertible debt at a conversion price (or other effective equity price) less than the Series C Applicable Conversion Price. c. Dividends, distributions or repurchases of any equity securities. d. Change of any right, preference or term of the Series C. e. Any amendment to the Charter or By-laws of the Company. f. Any significant sale of assets or transaction, which would result in a Change of Control. g. An increase in the number of directors constituting the Board of Directors to a number greater than seven.	This section is very important, as it mentions all of this Series' protective provisions. Without a minimum of a 50% Series C majority vote, none of these events (a-g) can take place. In this way, even if Series C owns a minority of the company, they can single-handedly veto any of the listed actions if such action were a threat or in some other way detrimental. Details on other voting thresholds will be found in the investment documents received during the diligence process.

ISSUER:	STARTUP, INC. (THE "COMPANY"), A DELAWARE CORPORATION.	COMMENTS
Board Approval:	The following action will require approval of a majority of the members of the Board, including the affirmative vote of the two directors designated by the holders of the Series C: 1. The incurrence of funded debt (excluding working capital borrowings based on accounts receivable). 2. The compensation of the CEO and CTO, and other key employees (and any other employee who is or becomes a holder of more than 5% of the Company's common stock on a fully diluted basis), as determined by the Compensation Committee.	
Registration Rights:	Upon the earlier of an IPO or the fifth anniversary of the closing, the holders of at least 30% of the Series C or the Conversion Stock (as defined below) may require that the Company file a registration statement covering common stock into which the Series C has been or will be converted (the "Conversion Stock") and which has been requested to be registered, subject to any then existing investment banker **lock-up period not to exceed 180 days**. The Company will not be obligated to consummate more than two demand registrations (at the Company's expense) under this provision in any 12-month period. The holders of Conversion Stock will be entitled to piggyback rights on registrations initiated by the Company or other shareholders on forms which permit the general sale of equity securities to the	All of the investors will be locked-up from selling the stock for a period of 180 after an IPO. This is a standard time period.

ISSUER:	STARTUP, INC. (THE "COMPANY"), A DELAWARE CORPORATION.	COMMENTS
Registration Rights, cont.:	shareholders, except as such registrations pertain to new issuances. The holders of Conversion Stock shall be entitled to two Form S-3 registration rights per year at such time as the Company is entitled to use Form S-3 provided that the aggregate offering involves more than $1,000,000. After an IPO, the Company will make requisite timely filings and otherwise use its best efforts to ensure that sales pursuant to use of Rules 144 or 144K are available to holders of Conversion Stock.	
Co-Sale Rights:	The holders of the Series C shall have the right, until a Qualified IPO, to sell their shares, on a pro rata basis, as part of any stock sales by or on behalf of other shareholders and affiliates which own 5% or more of the outstanding common stock.	Protection in the case that an insider (founder, C-Level executive, etc.) decides to sell their shares. Allows other investors to get out (sell) alongside the instigator.
Pre-emptive Rights:	The holders of the Series C shall have the right to purchase up to their pro rata share of subsequent equity financings of the Company, including convertible securities or securities with accompanying rights to acquire equity, subject to standard carve-outs for securities issued in non-financing transactions. Should any Investor not exercise their full pre-emptive rights, any allotment to such investor in excess of their purchase amount will be offered to other Investors on a pro rata basis.	Allows current investors to retain percentage of ownership by giving access to future funding rounds.
Employee Agreements::	Key employees (including all corporate officers) will enter into three-year non-competition agreements.	Good to have but tough to enforce (esp. in California)

ISSUER:	STARTUP, INC. (THE "COMPANY"), A DELAWARE CORPORATION.	COMMENTS
Key Man Life Insurance:	The Company will make best efforts to maintain term life insurance in the amount of $5 million on the life of CEO and CTO, with the Company as the beneficiary as long as they are employed.	
Board Representation:	The Investors will be entitled to two Board seats, with Board Observer rights for Strategic Investor #1. The Board of Directors will comprise seven members. If it has not already, the Company shall establish a Compensation Committee and Audit Committee of the Board. The Investors will have two seats on a three member Audit Committee and two seats on a three member Compensation Committee. The Company's Board of Directors will schedule meetings monthly until such time as the Investors determine monthly meetings are not required. The Company shall reimburse Investors' Directors for reasonable out-of-pocket travel and related expenses incurred to attend meetings.	Board seats are a liability to strategic investors, so observer rights bridge the gap. Board size should be actively managed, as any number larger than 7-9 tends to be counterproductve.
Warrants::	In the event the Company issues Warrants, options or other securities (collectively, the "Dilutive Securities") to other entities at or before any closing of this round, all such Dilutive Securities shall dilute the existing shareholders on a pro-rata basis, thereby adjusting the effective purchase price of the Series C to account for the dilutive effect.	

ISSUER:	STARTUP, INC. (THE "COMPANY"), A DELAWARE CORPORATION.	COMMENTS
Expenses:	The Company will pay reasonable legal fees of the counsel to the Investors' and due diligence expenses to VC Investor #3 and certain of the Investors, which, together, should not exceed $50,000.	$50K is on the high end. Don't get greedy here, and keep a handle over legal expenses. Every dollar that the Startup spends on lawyers is one less to grow its business.
Information Rights:	Monthly financial and operating statements within 30 days after the end of each monthly period with comparisons to budget. Annually, a budget and operating plan on a monthly basis for the coming fiscal year to be provided at least 30 days prior to each fiscal year end. A certified audit and management letter from an accounting firm satisfactory to the Investors within 90 days following each fiscal year end. Other relevant regulatory, sales and marketing information, including weekly sales reports.	Make sure that the Startup provides investors (who have a pre-determined minimum amount of share ownership) with adequate financial info on an ongoing basis. That said, do not make this an onerous task for the company. Remember, their energy should be spent on running the business, not printing weekly financials.
Representations:	Standard representations and warranties from the Company and the Investors.	Details in other investor documents.
Other Conditions:	Satisfactory completion of financial, operational and legal due diligence on the Company. The sale of the Series C will be pursuant to a Stock Purchase Agreement prepared by Investors' counsel with such terms and conditions as are reasonable and customary in transactions of this kind, including those which reflect this proposed term sheet. No material adverse change in the Company's business or financial prospects prior to closing.	Another "escape hatch" for investors. The deal will be signed subject to these conditions being met. So, if an ugly surprise is found during the diligence process, or the Startup finds itself embroiled in litigation over its IP (intellectual property), investors can gracefully back out of the deal.

Sample Capitalization Table

STARTUP, INC.—CAPITALIZATION TABLE (Common Stock)

COMMON STOCK								
NAME OF COMMON STOCKHOLDER	% SHARES & OPTIONS SUBJECT TO VESTING	RESTRICTED/ UNVESTED SHARES	% OWNED OF CLASS	TOTAL COMMON SHARES	NO. OF OPTIONS ON COMMON	NO. OF WARRANTS ON COMMON	% OWNED OF CLASS (DILUTED)	FULLY DILUTED COMMON SHRARES
FOUNDER #1						0	23.2%	5,000,000
FOUNDER #2 (CTO)	52.6%	500,000	42.5%	5,000,000	4,500,000	0	44.0%	9,500,000
CEO	93.5%	250,000	4.2%	500,000	3,375,000	0	18.0%	3,875,000
VP OF MARKETING & SALES	66.7%	25,000	0.4%	50,000	25,000	0	0.3%	75,000
FRIENDS & FAMILY INVESTORS	0.0%	0	10.4%	1,222,342	0	0	5.7%	1,222,342
OTHERS (EMPLOYEES)		0	0.0%	0	1,894,494	0	8.8%	1,894,494
TOTAL COMMON		775,000	100.0%	11,772,342	9,794,494	0	100.0%	21,566,836
TOTAL COMMON AUTHORIZED								59,852,057
TOTAL PREFERRED AUTHORIZED								36,444,782

OPTION POOL SUMMARY	% OF FULLY DILUTED POST MONEY SHARES	NO. OF OPTIONS ON COMMON
TOTAL AUTHORIZED OPTION POOL	19.4%	11,634,933
OPTIONS EXERCISED	0.0%	0
CURRENT OPTION POOL	19.4%	11,634,933
OPTIONS OUTSTANDING	16.4%	9,794,494
OPTIONS AVAILABLE FOR ISSUANCE	3.1%	1,840,439

STARTUP, INC.—CAPITALIZATION TABLE (Preferred Stock)

PREFERRED STOCK								
SERIES A PREFERRED	DATE OF FIRST CLOSING: PURCHASE PRICE/SERIES A SHARE:		5-JAN-00 $0.2500		CASH RAISED IN SERIES A: SHARES OF COMMON/SERIES A SHARE:			$810,227 1.000000
NAME OF INVESTOR		NO. OF A SHARES	% OWNED OF CLASS	COMMON EQUIVALENT A SHARES	NO. OF WARRANTS ON A SHARES	NO. OF COMMON EQUIV WARRANTS	% OWNED OF CLASS (DILUTED)	FULLY DILUTED COMMON EQUIV A SHARES
ANGEL INVESTOR #1					0	0	35.5%	1,150,000
ANGEL INVESTOR #2	35%	1,150,000	35.5%	1,150,000	0	0	29.0%	938,665
ANGEL INVESTOR #3	29%	938,665	29.0%	938,665	0	0	35.6%	1,152,242
OTHER A HOLDERS	36%	1,152,242	35.6%	1,152,242	0	0	0.0%	0
TOTAL SERIES A		0	0.0%	0	0	0	100.0%	3,240,907
TOTAL SERIES A AUTHORIZED		3,240,907	100.0%	3,240,907				3,240,907
SERIES B PREFERRED	DATE OF FIRST CLOSING: PURCHASE PRICE/SERIES B SHARE:		20-JUL-00 $0.5900		CASH RAISED IN SERIES B: SHARES OF COMMON/SERIES B SHARE:			$7,137,970 1.000000
NAME OF INVESTOR		NO. OF B SHARES	% OWNED OF CLASS	COMMON EQUIVALENT NO. OF SHARE	NO. OF WARRANTS ON B SHARES	NO. OF COMMON EQUIV WARRANTS	% OWNED OF CLASS (DILUTED)	FFULLY DILUTED COMMON EQUIV B SHARES
ANGEL INVESTOR #1		105,007	40.9%	105,007	0	0	0.9%	105,007
ANGEL INVESTOR #2		72,500	0.6%	72,500	0	0	0.6%	72,500
ANGEL INVESTOR #3		104,000	0.9%	104,000	0	0	0.9%	104,000
VC INVESTOR #1		7,043,741	58.2%	7,043,741	0	0	58.2%	7,043,741
VC INVESTOR #2		4,773,006	39.5%	4,773,006	0	0	39.5%	4,773,006
OTHER B HOLDERS		0	0.0%	0	0	0	0.0%	0
TOTAL SERIES B		12,098,254	100.0%	12,098,254	0	0	100.0%	12,098,254
TOTAL SERIES B AUTHORIZED								12,098,254

STARTUP, INC.—CAPITALIZATION TABLE (Preferred Stock)

PREFERRED STOCK								
SERIES C PREFERRED		DATE OF FIRST CLOSING: PURCHASE PRICE/SERIES C SHARE:		19-FEB-01 $1.2840	CASH RAISED IN SERIES C: SHARES OF COMMON/SERIES C SHARE:			$27,099,617 1.000000
NAME OF INVESTOR		NO. OF B SHARES	% OWNED OF CLASS	COMMON EQUIVALENT NO. OF SHARE	NO. OF WARRANTS ON C SHARES	NO. OF COMMON EQUIV WARRANTS	% OWNED OF CLASS (DILUTED)	FFULLY DILUTED COMMON EQUIV C SHARES
ANGEL INVESTOR #1		100,000	0.5%	100,000	0	0	0.5%	100,000
ANGEL INVESTOR #2		80,000	0.4%	80,000	0	0	0.4%	80,000
ANGEL INVESTOR #3		100,000	0.5%	100,000	0	0	0.5%	100,000
VC INVESTOR #1		1,500,000	7.1%	1,500,000	0	0	7.1%	1,500,000
VC INVESTOR #2		1,400,000	6.6%	1,400,000	0	0	6.6%	1,400,000
VC INVESTOR #3		8,000,000	37.9%	8,000,000	0	0	37.9%	8,000,000
VC INVESTOR #4		6,000,000	28.4%	6,000,000	0	0	28.4%	6,000,000
STRATEGIC INVESTOR #1		3,925,621	18.6%	3,925,621	0	0	18.6%	3,925,621
OTHERS		0	0.0%	0	0	0	0.0%	0
TOTAL SERIES C		21,105,621	100.0%	21,105,621	0	0	100.0%	21,105,621
TOTAL SERIES C AUTHORIZED								21,105,621

STARTUP, INC.—CAPITALIZATION TABLE (Summary Cap Table)

SUMMARY CAP TABLE		% OWNED OF COMPANY	COMMON EQUIV NO.	NO. OF OPTIONS IN OPTION POOL	NO. OF COMMON EQUIV WARRANTS	% OWNED OF COMPANY (DILUTED)	FULLY DILUTED COMMON EQUIV SHARES
TOTAL COMMON		24.4%	11,772,342	11,634,933	0	39.1%	23,407,275
TOTAL SERIES A		6.7%	3,240,907		0	5.4%	3,240,907
TOTAL SERIES B		25.1%	12,098,254		0	20.2%	12,098,254
TOTAL SERIES C		43.8%	21,105,621		0	35.3%	21,105,621
TOTAL DILUTED COMMON SHARE EQUIVALENTS		100.0%	48,217,124	11,634,933	0	100.0%	59,852,057
TOTAL DILUTED COMMON SHARE EQUIVALENTS (POST C)							59,852,057
PRICE PER SERIES C SHARE							$1.28
POST-MONEY VALUATION							$76,850,041
TOTAL DILUTED COMMON SHARE EQUIVALENTS (POST C)							59,852,057
TOTAL SHARES OF SERIES C (INCLUDING WARRANTS)							21,105,621
TOTAL DILUTED COMMON SHARE EQUIVALENTS (PRE C)							38,746,436
PRICE PER SERIES C SHARE							$1.28
PRE-MONEY VALUATION							$49,750,424

About the Authors

Oleg Kaganovich

Oleg Kaganovich has been both bootstrapping entrepreneur and venture capitalist. He has made strategic investments and acquisitions for Fortune 500 companies and investment banks, built financial analysis tools and developed company growth plans. After founding and growing a technology start-up in the mid-90's, Oleg attended both the Fletcher School of Law and Diplomacy and Columbia Business School, from which he holds an MBA. He worked as an investment banker with Black Emerald Capital on Wall Street and a venture capitalist with Sun Microsystems' venture group in Silicon Valley.

Now in Sacramento, he is the CEO of SARTA (Sacramento Area Regional Technology Alliance), a non-profit high tech association that works with public and private sector groups to drive entrepreneurial growth and attract investment capital to the region.

James Currier

James Currier is an eleven-year veteran of the venture capital industry. He was introduced to the business in 1991 by GTE New Ventures in California, and while at Battery Ventures in Boston, he co-founded "Capital Venture," the association of young venture capitalists. Currently the CEO of Tickle, Currier is a graduate of Harvard Business School (1999) and lives in San Francisco.

Joe Bel Bruno

Joe Bel Bruno is a New York-based journalist who has covered business and finance for the past ten years. He has worked for major publications in New York, Los Angeles and London, and was the recipient of two "Best in Business" awards from the Society of American Business Editors and Writers organization.